## MASTER THE™ DSST®

# Environmental Science Exam

## About Peterson's

Peterson's® has been your trusted educational publisher for over 50 years. It's a milestone we're quite proud of, as we continue to offer the most accurate, dependable, high-quality educational content in the field, providing you with everything you need to succeed. No matter where you are on your academic or professional path, you can rely on Peterson's for its books, online information, expert test-prep tools, the most up-to-date education exploration data, and the highest quality career success resources—everything you need to achieve your education goals. For our complete line of products, visit www.petersons.com.

For more information, contact Peterson's, 8740 Lucent Blvd., Suite 400, Highlands Ranch, CO 80129; 800-338-3282 Ext. 54229; or find us online at **www.petersons.com**.

# Contents

# Before You Begin

## HOW THIS BOOK IS ORGANIZED

Peterson's *Master the*™ *DSST® Environmental Science Exam* provides a diagnostic test, subject-matter review, and a post-test.

- **Diagnostic Test**—Twenty multiple-choice questions, followed by an answer key with detailed answer explanations
- **Assessment Grid**—A chart designed to help you identify areas that you need to focus on based on your test results
- **Subject-Matter Review**—General overview of the exam subject, followed by a review of the relevant topics and terminology covered on the exam
- **Post-test**—Sixty multiple-choice questions, followed by an answer key and detailed answer explanations

The purpose of the diagnostic test is to help you figure out what you know—or don't know. The twenty multiple-choice questions are similar to the ones found on the DSST exam, and they should provide you with a good idea of what to expect. Once you take the diagnostic test, check your answers to see how you did. Included with each correct answer is a brief explanation regarding why a specific answer is correct, and in many cases, why other options are incorrect. Use the assessment grid to identify the questions you miss so that you can spend more time reviewing that information later. As with any exam, knowing your weak spots greatly improves your chances of success.

Following the diagnostic test is a subject-matter review. The review summarizes the various topics covered on the DSST exam. Key terms are defined; important concepts are explained; and when appropriate, examples are provided. As you read the review, some of the information may seem familiar while other information may seem foreign. Again, take note of the unfamiliar because that will most likely cause you problems on the actual exam.

After studying the subject-matter review, you should be ready for the post-test. The post-test contains sixty multiple-choice items, and it will serve as a dry run for the real DSST exam. There are complete answer explanations at the end of the test.

## OTHER DSST® PRODUCTS BY PETERSON'S

Books, flashcards, practice tests, and videos available online at
**www.petersons.com/testprep/dsst**

- Art of the Western World
- Astronomy
- Business Mathematics
- Business Ethics and Society
- Civil War and Reconstruction
- Computing and Information Technology
- Criminal Justice
- Environmental Science
- Ethics in America
- Ethics in Technology
- Foundations of Education
- Fundamentals of College Algebra
- Fundamentals of Counseling
- Fundamentals of Cybersecurity
- General Anthropology
- Health and Human Development
- History of the Soviet Union
- History of the Vietnam War
- Human Resource Management
- Introduction to Business
- Introduction to Geography
- Introduction to Geology
- Introduction to Law Enforcement
- Introduction to World Religions
- Lifespan Developmental Psychology
- Math for Liberal Arts
- Management Information Systems
- Money and Banking
- Organizational Behavior
- Personal Finance
- Principles of Advanced English Composition
- Principles of Finance
- Principles of Public Speaking
- Principles of Statistics
- Principles of Supervision
- Substance Abuse
- Technical Writing

---

**Like what you see?** Get unlimited access to Peterson's full catalog of DSST practice tests, instructional videos, flashcards and more for **75% off the first month!** Go to **www.petersons.com/testprep/dsst** and use coupon code **DSST2020** at checkout. Offer expires July 1, 2021.

---

# Chapter 1

# All About the DSST® Exam

## WHAT IS DSST®?

Previously known as the DANTES Subject Standardized Tests, the DSST program provides the opportunity for individuals to earn college credit for what they have learned outside of the traditional classroom. Accepted or administered at more than 1,900 colleges and universities nationwide and approved by the American Council on Education (ACE), the DSST program enables individuals to use the knowledge they have acquired outside the classroom to accomplish their educational and professional goals.

## WHY TAKE A DSST® EXAM?

DSST exams offer a way for you to save both time and money in your quest for a college education. Why enroll in a college course in a subject you already understand? For over 30 years, the DSST program has offered the perfect solution for individuals who are knowledgeable in a specific subject and want to save both time and money. A passing score on a DSST exam provides physical evidence to universities of proficiency in a specific subject. More than 1,900 accredited and respected colleges and universities across the nation award undergraduate credit for passing scores on DSST exams. With the DSST program, individuals can shave months off the time it takes to earn a degree.

The DSST program offers numerous advantages for individuals in all stages of their educational development:

- Adult learners
- College students
- Military personnel

Adult learners desiring college degrees face unique circumstances—demanding work schedules, family responsibilities, and tight budgets. Yet adult learners also have years of valuable work experience that can frequently be applied toward a degree through the DSST program. For example, adult learners with on-the-job experience in business and management might be able to skip the Business 101 courses if they earn passing marks on DSST exams such as Introduction to Business and Principles of Supervision.

Adult learners can put their prior learning into action and move forward with more advanced course work. Adults who have never enrolled in a college course may feel a little uncertain about their abilities. If this describes your situation, then sign up for a DSST exam and see how you do. A passing score may be the boost you need to realize your dream of earning a degree. With family and work commitments, adult learners often feel they lack the time to attend college. The DSST program enables adult learners the unique opportunity to work toward college degrees without the time constraints of semester-long course work. DSST exams take two hours or less to complete. In one weekend, you could earn credit for multiple college courses.

The DSST exams also benefit students who are already enrolled in a college or university. With college tuition costs on the rise, most students face financial challenges. The fee for each DSST exam starts at $80 (plus administration fees charged by some testing facilities)—significantly less than the $750 average cost of a 3-hour college class. Maximize tuition assistance by taking DSST exams for introductory or mandatory course work. Once you earn a passing score on a DSST exam, you are free to move on to higher-level course work in that subject matter, take desired electives, or focus on courses in a chosen major.

Not only do college students and adult learners profit from DSST exams, but military personnel reap the benefits as well. If you are a member of the armed services at home or abroad, you can initiate your post-military career by taking DSST exams in areas with which you have experience. Military personnel can gain credit anywhere in the world, thanks to the fact that almost all of the tests are available through the internet at designated testing locations. DSST testing facilities are located at more than 500 military installations, so service members on active duty can get a jump-start on a post-military career with the DSST program. As an additional incentive, DANTES (Defense Activity for Non-Traditional Education Support) provides funding for DSST test fees for eligible members of the military.

More than 30 subject-matter tests are available in the fields of Business, Humanities, Math, Physical Science, Social Sciences, and Technology.

## Available DSST® Exams

| Business | Social Sciences |
|---|---|
| Business Ethics and Society | A History of the Vietnam War |
| Business Mathematics | Art of the Western World |
| Computing and Information Technology | Criminal Justice |
| Human Resource Management | Foundations of Education |
| Introduction to Business | Fundamentals of Counseling |
| Management Information Systems | General Anthropology |
| Money and Banking | History of the Soviet Union |
| Organizational Behavior | Introduction to Geography |
| Personal Finance | Introduction to Law Enforcement |
| Principles of Finance | Lifespan Developmental Psychology |
| Principles of Supervision | Substance Abuse |
| | The Civil War and Reconstruction |

| Humanities | Physical Sciences |
|---|---|
| Ethics in America | Astronomy |
| Introduction to World Religions | Environmental Science |
| Principles of Advanced English Composition | Health and Human Development |
| | Introduction to Geology |
| Principles of Public Speaking | |

| Math | Technology |
|---|---|
| Fundamentals of College Algebra | Ethics in Technology |
| Math for Liberal Arts | Fundamentals of Cybersecurity |
| Principles of Statistics | Technical Writing |

As you can see from the table, the DSST program covers a wide variety of subjects. However, it is important to ask two questions before registering for a DSST exam.

1. Which universities or colleges award credit for passing DSST exams?
2. Which DSST exams are the most relevant to my desired degree and my experience?

Knowing which universities offer DSST credit is important. In all likelihood, a college in your area awards credit for DSST exams, but find out before taking an exam by contacting the university directly. Then review the list of DSST exams to determine which ones are most relevant to the degree you are seeking and to your base of knowledge. Schedule an appointment with your college adviser to determine which exams best fit your degree program and which college courses the DSST exams can replace. Advisers should also be able to tell you the minimum score required on the DSST exam to receive university credit.

## DSST® TEST CENTERS

You can find DSST testing locations in community colleges and universities across the country. Check the DSST website (**www.getcollegecredit. com**) for a location near you or contact your local college or university to find out if the school administers DSST exams. Keep in mind that some universities and colleges administer DSST exams only to enrolled students. DSST testing is available to men and women in the armed services at more than 500 military installations around the world.

## HOW TO REGISTER FOR A DSST® EXAM

Once you have located a nearby DSST testing facility, you need to contact the testing center to find out the exam administration schedule. Many centers are set up to administer tests via the internet, while others use printed materials. Almost all DSST exams are available as online tests, but the method used depends on the testing center. The cost for each DSST exam starts at $80, and many testing locations charge a fee to cover their costs for administering the tests. Credit cards are the only accepted payment method for taking online DSST exams. Credit card, certified check, and money order are acceptable payment methods for paper-and-pencil tests.

Test takers are allotted two score reports—one mailed to them and another mailed to a designated college or university, if requested. Online tests generate unofficial scores at the end of the test session, while individuals taking paper tests must wait four to six weeks for score reports.

## PREPARING FOR A DSST® EXAM

Even though you are knowledgeable in a certain subject matter, you should still prepare for the test to ensure you achieve the highest score possible. The first step in studying for a DSST exam is to find out what will be on the specific test you have chosen. Information regarding test content is located on the DSST fact sheets, which can be downloaded at no cost from **www. getcollegecredit.com**. Each fact sheet outlines the topics covered on a subject-matter test, as well as the approximate percentage assigned to each topic. For example, questions on the Environmental Science exam are distributed in the following way: Ecological Concepts–30%, Environmental Impacts–25%, Environmental Management and Conservation–25%, and Social Processes and the Environment–20%.

In addition to the breakdown of topics on a DSST exam, the fact sheet also lists recommended reference materials. If you do not own the recommended books, then check college bookstores. Avoid paying high prices for new textbooks by looking online for used textbooks. Don't panic if you are unable to locate a specific textbook listed on the fact sheet; the textbooks are merely recommendations. Instead, search for comparable books used in university courses on the specific subject. Current editions are ideal, and it is a good idea to use at least two references when studying for a DSST exam. Of course, the subject matter provided in this book will be a sufficient review for most test takers. However, if you need additional information, then it is a good idea to have some of the reference materials at your disposal when preparing for a DSST exam.

Fact sheets include other useful information in addition to a list of reference materials and topics. Each fact sheet includes subject-specific sample questions like those you will encounter on the DSST exam. The sample questions provide an idea of the types of questions you can expect on the exam. Test questions are multiple-choice with one correct answer and three incorrect choices.

The fact sheet also includes information about the number of credit hours that ACE has recommended be awarded by colleges for a passing DSST exam score. However, you should keep in mind that not all universities and colleges adhere to the ACE recommendation for DSST credit hours. Some institutions require DSST exam scores higher than the minimum score recommended by ACE. Once you have acquired appropriate reference materials and you have the outline provided on the fact sheet, you are ready to start studying, which is where this book can help.

## TEST DAY

After reviewing the material and taking practice tests, you are finally ready to take your DSST exam. Follow these tips for a successful test day experience.

1. **Arrive on time.** Not only is it courteous to arrive on time to the DSST testing facility, but it also allows plenty of time for you to take care of check-in procedures and settle into your surroundings.

2. **Bring identification.** DSST test facilities require that candidates bring a valid government-issued identification card with a current photo and signature. Acceptable forms of identification include a current driver's license, passport, military identification card, or state-issued identification card. Individuals who fail to bring proper identification to the DSST testing facility will not be allowed to take an exam.

3. **Bring the right supplies.** If your exam requires the use of a calculator, you may bring a calculator that meets the specifications. For paper-based exams, you may also bring No. 2 pencils with an eraser and black ballpoint pens. Regardless of the exam methodology, you are NOT allowed to bring reference or study materials, scratch paper, or electronics such as cell phones, personal handheld devices, cameras, alarm wrist watches, or tape recorders to the testing center.

4. **Take the test.** During the exam, take the time to read each question-and-answer option carefully. Eliminate the choices you know are incorrect to narrow the number of potential answers. If a question completely stumps you, take an educated guess and move on—remember that DSSTs are timed; you will have 2 hours to take the exam.

With the proper preparation, DSST exams will save you both time and money. So join the thousands of people who have already reaped the benefits of DSST exams and move closer than ever to your college degree.

## ENVIRONMENTAL SCIENCE EXAM FACTS

The DSST® Environmental Science exam consists of 100 multiple-choice questions designed to evaluate your knowledge in a specific area of physical science which includes ecological concepts (ecosystems, global ecology, and food chains and food webs), habitat destruction, environmental management and conservation, and social processes and the environment.

**Area or Course Equivalent:** Environmental Science
**Level:** Lower-level baccalaureate
**Amount of Credit:** 3 Semester Hours
**Minimum Score:** 400
**Source:** https://www.getcollegecredit.com/wp-content/assets/fact-sheets/EnvironmentalScience.pdf

## I. Ecological Concepts – 30%

    a. Ecosystems

    b. Organism Relationships

    c. Biodiversity

    d. Trophic relationships (e.g. food chain; food web)

    e. Energy flows and cycles

    f. Biomes

    g. Population biology

    h. Evolution

    i. Ecological succession

## II. Environmental Impacts – 25%

    a. Human population dynamics

    b. Global climate change

    c. Pollution – physical, chemical, and biological aspects

    d. Agricultural

    e. Industrial

    f. Habitat destruction

    g. Land degradation

## III. Environmental Management and Conservation – 25%

    a. Renewable and nonrenewable resources

    b. Agricultural practices

    c. Pesticides and pest control

    d. Soil conservation and land use practices

    e. Air pollution control

    f. Water quality and supply

    g. Wastewater treatment

    h. Solid and hazardous waste

    i. Environmental risk assessment

**IV. Social Processes and the Environment – 20%**

    a. Environmental justice

    b. Policy, planning and decision making

    c. Global environmental governance

    d. Differing culture and societal values

# Chapter 2

# Environmental Science Diagnostic Test

## DIAGNOSTIC TEST ANSWER SHEET

1. Ⓐ Ⓑ Ⓒ Ⓓ        8. Ⓐ Ⓑ Ⓒ Ⓓ        15. Ⓐ Ⓑ Ⓒ Ⓓ

2. Ⓐ Ⓑ Ⓒ Ⓓ        9. Ⓐ Ⓑ Ⓒ Ⓓ        16. Ⓐ Ⓑ Ⓒ Ⓓ

3. Ⓐ Ⓑ Ⓒ Ⓓ        10. Ⓐ Ⓑ Ⓒ Ⓓ       17. Ⓐ Ⓑ Ⓒ Ⓓ

4. Ⓐ Ⓑ Ⓒ Ⓓ        11. Ⓐ Ⓑ Ⓒ Ⓓ       18. Ⓐ Ⓑ Ⓒ Ⓓ

5. Ⓐ Ⓑ Ⓒ Ⓓ        12. Ⓐ Ⓑ Ⓒ Ⓓ       19. Ⓐ Ⓑ Ⓒ Ⓓ

6. Ⓐ Ⓑ Ⓒ Ⓓ        13. Ⓐ Ⓑ Ⓒ Ⓓ       20. Ⓐ Ⓑ Ⓒ Ⓓ

7. Ⓐ Ⓑ Ⓒ Ⓓ        14. Ⓐ Ⓑ Ⓒ Ⓓ

# ENVIRONMENTAL SCIENCE DIAGNOSTIC TEST

**Directions:** Carefully read each of the following 20 questions. Choose the best answer to each question and fill in the corresponding circle on the answer sheet. The Answer Key and Explanations can be found following this Diagnostic Test.

1. America's first environmental legislation was passed in response to what environmental issue?

    **A.** Water pollution
    **B.** Persistent pesticides
    **C.** The illegal wildlife trade
    **D.** Overfishing

2. Which process is a method used only in making ocean water suitable for drinking?

    **A.** Disinfecting
    **B.** Desalination
    **C.** Filtering
    **D.** Cleansing

3. What is one of the greatest benefits of high species diversity to an ecosystem?

    **A.** Diversity enhances the monetary value of an ecosystem.
    **B.** Diversity increases the stability of an ecosystem.
    **C.** Diversity increases the amount of energy available in an ecosystem.
    **D.** Diversity increases available habitats in an ecosystem.

4. All of the following are ways to combat air pollution from transportation EXCEPT:

    **A.** Compact development
    **B.** Fuel efficiency standards
    **C.** Public parking
    **D.** Public transportation

5. Which of the following terms describes how water is taken up into the atmosphere from a lake?

   **A.** Transpiration
   **B.** Evaporation
   **C.** Condensation
   **D.** Precipitation

6. What is it called when two individuals of the same species have different physical characteristics, and one is able to live long enough to reproduce and the other is not?

   **A.** Macroevolution
   **B.** Adaptation
   **C.** Natural selection
   **D.** Coevolution

7. Which of the following occupies the first trophic level?

   **A.** Consumers
   **B.** Carnivores
   **C.** Herbivores
   **D.** Producers

8. Industrial waste containing dioxins would be considered

   **A.** medical waste.
   **B.** hazardous waste.
   **C.** recyclable waste.
   **D.** solid waste.

9. The excessive growth of algae in a freshwater ecosystem is called

   **A.** water pollution.
   **B.** algaefication.
   **C.** eutrophication.
   **D.** deforestation.

10. Which of the following is an example of a species found in a pioneer community?

    **A.** Lichen
    **B.** Wildflowers
    **C.** Fungi
    **D.** Bacteria

11. The development of agriculture began with the concept of

    A. hunting and gathering.
    B. increasing food volume.
    C. manipulating plants and soil.
    D. clearing large plots of land.

12. In 1898, a Swedish scientist predicted that carbon dioxide emissions from excessive burning of fossil fuels could lead to

    A. the greenhouse effect.
    B. the Industrial Revolution.
    C. air pollution.
    D. global warming.

13. Which of the following is a possible way to protect rangelands from erosion and fire?

    A. Raise sheep instead of cattle.
    B. Rotate grazing areas.
    C. Plant fire-resistant vegetation.
    D. Only graze animals on steep slopes.

14. Which process removes large particles from wastewater?

    A. Primary sewage treatment
    B. Secondary sewage treatment
    C. Tertiary sewage treatment
    D. Quaternary sewage treatment

15. The first phase of population growth is often called the

    A. exponential phase.
    B. equilibrium phase.
    C. deceleration phase.
    D. lag phase.

16. What event was considered the first environmental justice action in the United States?

    A. The Flint water crisis
    B. The 1968 Memphis Sanitation Strike
    C. The Lacey Act
    D. The 1963 March on Washington

17. Which of the following is true of the Paris Agreement?

    **A.** It was signed in 2017.
    **B.** The United States is not a signatory.
    **C.** The agreement is voluntary.
    **D.** The agreement has strict enforcement mechanisms.

18. Which of the following is a type of volatile organic compound?

    **A.** Lead
    **B.** Sulfur dioxide
    **C.** Hydrocarbons
    **D.** Particulate matter

19. Designing industrial production methods with biological impacts in mind is called

    **A.** Industrial Revolution.
    **B.** industrial ecology.
    **C.** biological revolution.
    **D.** ecological diversity.

20. In 1970, Congress established

    **A.** Earth Day.
    **B.** the World Health Organization.
    **C.** the Environmental Protection Agency.
    **D.** Agenda 21.

# ANSWER KEY AND EXPLANATIONS

| | | | | |
|---|---|---|---|---|
| 1. C | 5. B | 9. C | 13. B | 17. D |
| 2. B | 6. C | 10. A | 14. A | 18. C |
| 3. B | 7. D | 11. C | 15. D | 19. B |
| 4. C | 8. B | 12. D | 16. B | 20. C |

1. **The correct answer is C.** America's first environmental law, the Lacey Act, prohibits trade in illegal animal, fish, or plants and was passed in response to an out-of-control poaching problem. Choice A was addressed much later by the Clean Water Act. Choice B is covered by a range of regulations overseen by the EPA. Overfishing (choice D) is addressed in the United States by a more recent law called the Magnuson-Stevens Fishery Conservation and Management Act.

2. **The correct answer is B.** The process of desalination is necessary to remove the salts from ocean water so that it can be used as a source of drinking water. Choice A is incorrect because all water sources are disinfected with chlorine, UV light, or ozone. Choice C is incorrect because filtering is a process that is performed on all drinking water supplies. Choice D is incorrect because all water is cleansed before it is safe for drinking.

3. **The correct answer is B.** More diverse ecosystems have more connections among organisms and are more resistant to disturbance. Choice A is incorrect since while increased value to humans might be a result of biodiversity, increased value is of no benefit to the ecosystem itself. Choice C is incorrect because the energy available will depend on the producers and access to sunlight or appropriate chemicals, not on diversity. Choice D is incorrect because more habitats generally lead to more diversity, not the other way around.

4. **The correct answer is C.** Public parking, or any other development that encourages driving, is not likely to have much effect on vehicle emissions. There may be a slight reduction since people do not have to circle for parking, but the effect will be small compared to the other choices. Compact development (choice A) reduces emissions by reducing the distances people need to drive. Choice B allows a car to go farther for the same amount of fuel, reducing emissions per trip. Choice D provides an efficient alternative to personal cars, reducing emissions.

5. **The correct answer is B.** Evaporation occurs in bodies of water as water on the surface is changed into water vapor, a gas, and released into the atmosphere. Choice A is incorrect because transpiration is the process by which plants lose water through the stomata in their leaves. This results in the release of water into the atmosphere, but through plants, not a body of water. Choice C is incorrect because condensation is the change from a gas to a liquid, and it involves water already in the atmosphere. Choice D is incorrect because precipitation comes from water already in the atmosphere that falls to the earth.

6. **The correct answer is C.** Natural selection, also referred to as survival of the fittest, occurs when one member of a species is able to survive and reproduce and another one dies before reproducing. Choice A is incorrect because macroevolution refers to large-scale evolutionary changes over a long period of time. Choice B is incorrect because adaptations are changes in an organism or species that don't affect their ability to survive and reproduce. Choice D is incorrect because coevolution is when two or more species interact and exert selective pressure on one another, which can lead to adaptations and evolutionary changes in both species.

7. **The correct answer is D.** Producers occupy the first trophic level and obtain energy from the sun. This energy is converted and some of it is passed on to other species at higher trophic levels. Choice A is incorrect because consumers occupy the second trophic level and above. Choice B is incorrect because carnivores occupy either the third or fourth trophic level. Choice C is incorrect because herbivores occupy the second trophic level.

**8. The correct answer is B.** Dioxins are toxic chemicals, and industrial waste containing dioxins is considered to be hazardous waste. Choice A is incorrect because dioxins are environmental pollutants and are not considered medical waste or biohazardous material. Choice C is incorrect because dioxins are not a recyclable material. Choice D is incorrect because dioxins are an organic chemical compound and are considered hazardous waste, not solid waste.

**9. The correct answer is C.** The excessive growth of algae and aquatic plants due to added nutrients in the water is called eutrophication. Choice A is incorrect because although nutrients can cause water pollution, the excessive growth of algae caused by added nutrients is more specifically called eutrophication. Choice B is incorrect because algaefication is not a term used by environmental scientists. Choice D is incorrect because deforestation refers to activities that destroy forest environments and does not refer to algae growth.

**10. The correct answer is A.** Lichens are a type of pioneer organism that establish themselves on rocks and contribute to the formation of a thin layer of soil, so other organisms can grow. Choice B is incorrect because wildflowers need soil to establish and grow. Choice C is incorrect because fungi need to grow on organic material. Choice D is incorrect because bacteria are introduced at later stages of succession.

**11. The correct answer is C.** The origin of agricultural practices began with the concept of manipulating plants and soil to grow desired crops. Choice A is incorrect because hunting and gathering of food came before the advent of agricultural practices. Choice B is incorrect because increasing food volume was a result of the Agricultural Revolution, not the beginning of it. Choice D is incorrect because clearing large plots of land and manipulating plants and soil were concepts that came after the advent of agriculture.

12. **The correct answer is D.** During the rise of the Industrial Revolution, Svante August Arrhenius warned that an increase in carbon dioxide could lead to an increase in Earth's temperatures, an effect that we refer to as global warming. Choices A, B, and C are incorrect because these aren't what Arrhenius warned against.

13. **The correct answer is B.** Rotating the areas where livestock graze will allow the plants to regrow before they are overgrazed. Choice A will not help since grazing too many livestock of any species will result in range destruction. Choice C is not a good solution since it is the grazing that increases fire risk in the first place. Choice D will not help since it does not reduce the number of animals grazed in a particular area, and may make things worse since slopes are more vulnerable to erosion than are flat areas.

14. **The correct answer is A.** The removal of large particles from sewage wastewater by a process of filtering the water through screens takes place during primary sewage treatment. Choice B is incorrect because secondary sewage treatment involves the dissolving away of organic materials with microorganisms. Choice C is incorrect because tertiary sewage treatment involves the removal of inorganic nutrients such as nitrogen and phosphorus. Choice D is incorrect because there are only three sewage treatment steps, not four.

15. **The correct answer is D.** The first part of a population growth curve is often referred to as the lag phase because populations grow very slowly at first; the process of reproduction takes some time to get started. Choice A is incorrect because the exponential growth phase is the time of a high growth rate of a population. This usually follows the initial lag phase. Choice B is incorrect because the equilibrium phase occurs when a population is relatively stable, after the exponential growth phase. Choice C is incorrect because the deceleration phase is when the birth and death rates become equal and the population stops growing.

16. **The correct answer is B.** The 1968 Memphis Sanitation Strike combined civil rights and environmental activism and is considered to be the first environmental justice action in the United States. Choice A is incorrect since the Flint water crisis occurred in 2014, decades after activists first took notice of environmental justice issues. Choice C was an early act of legislation and was not connected to environmental justice. Choice D was a milestone in the civil rights movement but the environment was not one of the major concerns raised at the event.

17. **The correct answer is D.** The Paris Agreement, or Paris Accord, is a purely voluntary agreement that requires all signatory nations to devise their own means to reduce their greenhouse gas emissions. There is no provision to enforce the reduction target. Choice A is incorrect since the agreement was completed in 2016. Choice B is incorrect since the United States withdrew from the Paris Agreement in 2017. Choice C is incorrect since the agreement really is purely voluntary.

18. **The correct answer is C.** Volatile organic compounds are mostly composed of hydrogen and carbon atoms, and they are, therefore, called hydrocarbons. Choice A is incorrect because lead is not an organic compound. Choice B is incorrect because sulfur dioxide is not considered a hydrocarbon. Choice D is incorrect because particulate matter is a solid form of air pollution, not a volatile gaseous form.

19. **The correct answer is B.** During the mid-1990s, a concept called industrial ecology emerged, which aimed to integrate industry more closely with biology and limit ecological impacts. Choice A is incorrect because the Industrial Revolution marks the advent of the use of coal as a fuel source to power machinery used in the production of goods. Choice C is incorrect because there is no such thing as the biological revolution. Choice D is incorrect because ecological diversity concerns living organisms and ecosystems, not industrial production.

**20. The correct answer is C.** The Environmental Protection Agency (EPA) was established by the U.S. Congress in 1970. Choice A is incorrect because although the first Earth Day was held in 1970, it is not a government-sponsored organization. Choice B is incorrect because the World Health Organization (WHO) is an international organization that was established by the United Nations. Choice D is incorrect because Agenda 21 is a statement of principles for the management of global environmental issues.

# DIAGNOSTIC TEST ASSESSMENT GRID

Now that you've completed the diagnostic test and read through the answer explanations, you can use your results to target your studying. Find the question numbers from the diagnostic test that you answered incorrectly and highlight or circle them below. Then focus extra attention on the sections dealing with those topics.

| Environmental Science | | |
|---|---|---|
| **Content Area** | **Topic** | **Question #** |
| Ecological Concepts | • Ecosystems<br>• Organism Relationship<br>• Trophic Relationships<br>• Energy flows and cycles<br>• Biomes<br>• Population biology<br>• Evolution<br>• Ecological succession | 3, 5, 6, 7, 10, 15 |
| Environmental Impacts | • Human population dynamics<br>• Global climate change<br>• Pollution—physical, chemical, and biological aspects<br>• Agricultural<br>• Industrial<br>• Habit destruction<br>• Land degradation | 9, 12, 13, 18, 19 |
| Environmental Management and Conservation | • Renewable and nonrenewable resources<br>• Agricultural practices<br>• Pesticides and pest control<br>• Soil conservation and land use practices<br>• Air pollution control<br>• Water quality and supply<br>• Wastewater treatment<br>• Solid and hazardous waste<br>• Environmental risk assessment | 2, 4, 8, 11, 14 |
| Social Processes and the Environment | • Environmental justice<br>• Policy, planning, and decision making<br>• Global and environmental governance<br>• Differing culture and societal values | 1, 16, 17, 20 |

# Chapter 3

# Environmental Science Subject Review

## ECOLOGICAL CONCEPTS

Approximately 30 percent of the questions on the DSST® Environmental Science exam will cover topics under the umbrella of ecological concepts. Ecology is the study of how organisms interact with one another and their nonliving surroundings. Ecologists study the ways in which organisms have adapted to their surroundings, how they make use of their surroundings, and how an area is altered by the presence and activities of organisms. When these interactions are examined at a global scale, it is called global ecology.

## Ecosystems

Even though ecosystems are a complex network of interrelationships between organisms, all ecosystems have two main components:

- **Abiotic** factors are "nonliving" factors such as physical or chemical conditions within an environment. For example, in a salt marsh ecosystem, the abiotic factors would include climate, weather, water temperature, salinity, pH, soil composition, and oxygen content of the water and mud.
- **Biotic** factors are "living" factors, including all the living organisms within an ecosystem. In a salt marsh ecosystem, the biotic factors would include marsh grass, shrubs, and all plant life; fish, worms, insects, shellfish, crabs, and birds; and microorganisms such as bacteria and plankton.

Biotic factors can be organized into a hierarchy from the lowest level to the highest level:

1. **Organisms:** Individual life forms. For example, in a salt marsh, some organisms are marsh grass, flounder, and fiddler crabs.

2. **Species:** A population of organisms potentially capable of reproducing naturally among themselves to produce offspring that can also reproduce. All members of a species share similar behaviors, genetic structure, and appearance. For example, fiddler crabs are one species that inhabits salt marshes.
3. **Population:** A group of the same species living in the same geographic region at the same time. For example, the fiddler crabs living in a salt marsh in Maryland are a separate population from fiddler crabs living in a salt marsh in Delaware.
4. **Community:** All of the interacting populations of different species that live in a given area at the same time. In a salt marsh ecosystem, fiddler crabs, fish, birds, and plants all form a community.

Noting the above information, it is easy to see that an ecosystem is a community of different species that interact with one another and with surrounding abiotic factors. The interaction of both biotic and abiotic factors allows an ecosystem to respond to changes in the environment. When these interactions are examined at a global scale, it is called global ecology.

## Organism Relationships

Each species in an ecosystem has a specific role, or job, within the community. Examining the roles of species can help determine how they might interact. The functional role of each species in an ecosystem is its **niche**. A niche consists of all the physical, chemical, and biological conditions that a particular species requires in order to survive and reproduce within a given ecosystem. A description of an organism's niche always includes all the ways in which it affects other organisms and how it may modify its physical surroundings.

Ecologists have identified three general types of organism-to-organism interactions that take place in all ecosystems:

1. **Predation:** One organism, known as the predator, kills and eats another organism, known as the prey. The predator benefits from this relationship, and the prey is harmed. To succeed, predators have adapted several strategies, such as speed, stealth, or the ability to build a trap for their prey. At the same time, many prey species have adapted characteristics that help them to avoid predation. These characteristics include keen senses, the ability to camouflage, and the ability to remain motionless to avoid detection.
2. **Competition:** Within an ecosystem, many species compete for limited resources such as food, water, sunlight, and territory. Competition is classified as **intraspecific** if it occurs between members of the same species, and

**interspecific** if it occurs between members of different species. Whichever organism is less harmed by the competition is the winner. One organism may win out over another by one of two ways:

- In **interference**, one organism limits the access of another species to a resource.
- In **exploitation**, two or more organisms have equal access to a resource, but one uses it more quickly and efficiently than the other.

The competitive exclusion principle states that no two species can occupy the same ecological niche in the same place at the same time. The more similar two species are, the fiercer their competition will become.

3. **Symbiosis:** A close, long-lasting physical relationship between two species. The two species are in close physical contact, and at least one of them derives some benefit from the relationship. There are three different categories of symbiotic relationships:

- Parasitism: A relationship in which one organism, the parasite, lives in or on another organism, the host. The parasite generally derives nourishment from the host, and the host is harmed, or more rarely eventually killed, by the parasite.
- Commensalism: A relationship between organisms in which one organism benefits and the other is not affected.
- Mutualism: A relationship between organisms that is beneficial to both organisms. In many cases of mutualism, the species cannot live without each another.

## Biodiversity

**Biodiversity** is a term used to describe the diversity (variations) of genes, species, and ecosystems within a region. **Genetic diversity** is a term used to describe the number of different kinds of genes that are present in a given population. A high genetic diversity means there is a large amount of variation in structure and function among a population, and a low genetic diversity indicates that the population is almost all uniform in its traits. Genetic diversity is dependent on chromosomal mutations, migration of individuals or a population, sexual reproduction, population size, and selective breeding.

Species diversity is a measure of the number of various species within a given area. Some localities have high species diversity (a large number of species) and others have low species diversity. Factors that affect species diversity are the size of the area, human activities, and evolutionary and geological history of an area. Generally, but not always, the larger the area, the more species are present. A greater number of habitats in a given area will usually result in greater diversity.

Greater diversity means more connections among species and greater stability; more diverse ecosystems recover more quickly from disturbances such as natural disasters and are more resistant to damage from introduced non-native organisms.

Ecosystem diversity is a measure of the number of different kinds of ecosystems present in a given area. Even if areas appear to have general similarities (for example, all deserts have low rainfall), there are specific organisms that live in each ecosystem that create diversity.

## Trophic Relationships

Ecologists divide organisms into four broad categories. Each level in the first two categories is known as a trophic level.

1. **Producers:** Organisms that are able to use sources of energy to make complex, organic molecules from simple inorganic substances in their environment. All other organisms rely on producers as a food source, either directly or indirectly. Producers are the first, or lowest trophic level.
2. **Consumers:** Organisms that require organic matter as a food source. They consume organic matter to obtain energy and organic materials that will help to build and maintain their own bodies. Consumers can be further divided based on what they eat:
     ◉ Primary Consumers: These are organisms that eat producers and are also known as herbivores. Ecosystems generally have a large number of herbivores.
     ◉ Secondary Consumers: These are organisms that eat other consumers and are also known as carnivores. Some carnivores primarily eat herbivores, while others consume carnivores and herbivores.
     ◉ Tertiary Consumers: A carnivore that feeds on secondary consumers or below; these generally have few if any predators.
3. **Omnivores:** These include both producers (plants) and consumers (animals) in their diet. In trophic terms, omnivores feed at multiple trophic levels.
4. **Decomposers:** These are organisms, considered to be a type of consumer, that use nonliving, organic matter as a source of energy and material to build their bodies. When an organism sheds, excretes waste products, or dies, it provides a source of food for decomposers.

All ecosystems are stable, self-regulating units, but they are continually changing. The organisms within an ecosystem are continually growing, reproducing, dying, and decaying. Ecosystems must have a continuous input of energy to remain stable. This energy is usually provided by the sun, but there are unusual ecosystems in the deep sea where energy is derived from chemicals (chemosynthesis).

Producers occupy the first trophic level. Herbivores occupy the second trophic level. The third trophic level consists of carnivores that eat herbivores, and the fourth trophic level consists of carnivores that eat other carnivores.

Omnivores, parasites, and scavengers occupy a different trophic level depending on what they are eating at any given time. For example, if you eat a salad, you feed at the second trophic level;, and if you eat a steak, you feed at the third trophic level. Decomposers process food from all trophic levels.

## Food Chains and Food Webs

A food chain describes the relationship of organisms in an ecosystem in terms of who eats whom. Members of a food chain occupy different trophic levels, and energy passes from one organism to another as they are eaten. For example, the leaves on a tree growing beside a lake would take energy from the sun and provide a food source for insects. These insects are a food source for spiders living in the tree. If a spider falls from the tree into the pond, it can then be eaten by a frog. In turn, this frog may be eaten by a bass that is then caught by a fisherman. In the next step of this food chain, the fish is then consumed by humans. The typical order in a five-step food chain is as follows:

> producer → primary consumer → secondary consumer → tertiary consumer → decomposers

Because most consumers eat two or more types of organisms at different trophic levels, multiple food chains can overlap and intersect to form a food web. Complex food webs are more stable than simple food chains, but in this network of interactions, several organisms can be affected if one key organism is reduced in number.

## Energy Flows and Cycles

Energy in an ecosystem is not static, it moves through the food chains and out through the food webs in a very specific direction. In almost all ecosystems, energy supplied by the sun is used to carry out **photosynthesis**—the chemical process by which water and carbon dioxide are converted into glucose and oxygen—by producers, e.g. plants, algae, or phytoplankton. Producers obtain energy from a source like the sun, and this energy is then passed through the producers to consumers and decomposers. The glucose is a sugar that is incorporated into the producer's body. Consumers that eat the plants transfer the plant, and the energy used to grow that plant, into their own bodies and so on up each trophic level. Each transfer of energy to another trophic level is called **trophic transfer**.

The available energy decreases as the trophic level increases; some energy is lost to the environment as heat with each trophic transfer. The decreasing amount of available energy at each level is known as the **energy pyramid**. When an organism dies, some of the energy it contained becomes part of the decomposer's body. The rest is returned to the ecosystem as **detritus**, a rich food source for plants and some animals.

## Nutrient Cycles

Nutrients also flow through ecosystems. As matter flows through an eco-system, it gets recycled. Many chemicals that are important to sustain life and the growth of organisms cycle between organisms, the atmosphere, the oceans, and Earth's crust. These chemicals include carbon, nitrogen, oxygen, phosphorus, sulfur, and water. The cycles of these chemicals are called **biogeochemical cycles**. Biogeochemical cycles involve multiple ecosystems and have global effects.

**Carbon Cycle:** Carbon is the main element in all living organisms. It is also found in the atmosphere as carbon dioxide and in the oceans and rocks as carbonates. The carbon cycle includes processes and pathways that capture inorganic carbon-based molecules and convert them into organic carbon-based molecules that can be used by organisms. The same carbon atoms are used over and over. Carbon dioxide is fixed into plants and microorganisms through photosynthesis. Carbon passes through the food chains and webs as consumers eat. Fixed carbon in food and waste is broken down through respiration. Carbon from decomposing matter gets released back into soil. Carbon dioxide from the atmosphere moves into oceans. Sediment contains carbonate and compresses over time to form sedimentary rocks. Geological forces such as earthquakes and volcanoes return carbon from rocks back into the atmosphere. Human activity such as burning fossil fuels and raising farm animals like pigs and cattle also releases large quantities of carbon dioxide into the atmosphere.

**Nitrogen Cycle:** The major source of nitrogen is Earth's atmosphere. It is 78 percent nitrogen gas. Living organisms cannot utilize nitrogen gas, so it must first be converted to another chemical form, such a nitrates or nitrites. The chemical conversions in the nitrogen cycle are made by bacteria and other microorganisms. There are five important steps in the nitrogen cycle:

1. Nitrogen gas must be made into a chemically usable form by the process known as nitrogen fixation. Nitrogen-fixing bacteria can convert nitrogen gas from the atmosphere into ammonia, which contains nitrogen, in the soil. Nitrifying bacteria in the soil convert ammonia to nitrates and nitrates. This process is called **nitrification**.
2. Plants take up nitrates from the soil and incorporate them into amino acids. Animals eat the plants and incorporate the ingested nitrogen from plant amino acids into their own amino acids, proteins, nucleic acids, and other nitrogen-containing organic molecules. This process is called **assimilation**.
3. After animals and plants die, decomposers convert their nitrogen-containing organic molecules back into ammonia and return it to the soil. This process is called **ammonification**.
4. The ammonia can be used directly by many types of plants. Nitrifying bacteria in the soil are able to convert ammonia to nitrite and nitrate. Under conditions where oxygen is absent, denitrifying bacteria are able to convert nitrite to nitrogen gas. This process is called **denitrification**.
5. The nitrogen gas is eventually released back into the atmosphere, where it can then reenter the nitrogen cycle.

**Phosphorus Cycle:** Phosphorus is another element that is common to living organisms. It is present in many important biological molecules, such as DNA and cell membranes. Phosphorus containing ATP and ADP are important molecules for storing and utilizing energy in living organisms. Many enzymes require a phosphate group for activation or inactivation. Unlike carbon and nitrogen, phosphorus is not present in the atmosphere, so the phosphorus cycle is limited to soil and water. The major form of phosphorus is the mineral apatite, which is found in rocks and phosphate deposits. The weathering of phosphate rocks leaches phosphate into soil. Then plants take up phosphorus from the soil and incorporate it into their tissue. Animals eat the plants and take up the phosphate. When plants and animals die, decomposers release phosphate back into the soil. Animal excretion also contains phosphate that is released back into the soil.

**Sulfur Cycle:** Sulfur is important for the production of proteins because the amino acids cysteine and cystine contain sulfur. Sulfur is mainly found in rocks and soil as sulfate minerals. There is also sulfur in the atmosphere in the form of hydrogen sulfide. Weathering exposes sulfates from rocks, which are deposited into soil and aquatic ecosystems. Plants and other photosynthetic organisms take up and assimilate the sulfates into their tissue. Then animals eat plants and assimilate sulfates into their tissue. Death and decomposition of plants and animals convert organic sulfates into inorganic sulfates. Animal excretions also add sulfates to water and soil. Inorganic sulfates are then recycled. During decomposition in both soil and water, sulfates are converted into hydrogen sulfide gas that can escape into the atmosphere, water, soil, and marine sediment. Hydrogen sulfide gas can also come from volcanoes and power plant emissions.

**Oxygen Cycle:** Molecular oxygen is critical for all living things. It is a by-product of photosynthesis and a necessary reactant for cellular respiration. Biological and chemical processes help to recycle oxygen on Earth. The main supply of oxygen is our atmosphere. Oxygen cycles through the atmosphere, living organisms, and Earth's crust. Oxygen is removed from the atmosphere by chemically reacting with rocks and minerals exposed to weathering. Oxygen is also removed from the atmosphere through respiration of living organisms. Sunlight breaks down water into hydrogen and oxygen, and oxygen is released into the atmosphere. Photosynthesis also breaks down water into hydrogen and oxygen, releasing oxygen into the atmosphere.

**Hydrologic Cycle:** Water cycles between the atmosphere and Earth's surface and underground, and it exists in three states: solid, liquid, and gas. This cycle is primarily driven by the sun's energy. Water is stored in the atmosphere as water vapor (gas), on Earth's surface as a liquid (lakes, oceans, rivers, streams) or a solid (ice, glaciers), and in the ground as a liquid (groundwater) or a solid (ice in the form of permafrost). Energy from the sun is the source of power that drives the water cycle. Water can move among all these sites in six different ways:

1. Water moves from its liquid or solid state on Earth's surface to the atmosphere into its gaseous state through evaporation and sublimation.
2. Groundwater moves into the atmosphere through plants during the process of transpiration, a part of photosynthesis.
3. Thermal energy from the sun is absorbed by Earth's surface and snow and ice melt into liquid water. This water either flows into lakes, oceans, rivers, or streams or is absorbed as groundwater.
4. Energy released by water vapor in the atmosphere causes precipitation, and liquid water returns to Earth's surface.

5. Once on Earth's surface, water flows through porous surfaces and into liquid groundwater storage.
6. Liquid groundwater can also flow back to Earth's surface and into streams, lakes, rivers, and oceans.

Humans significantly impact the flow of all the biogeochemical cycles through the burning of fossil fuels, the conversions of natural ecosystems to agricultural land, agricultural runoff, and industrialization.

## Biomes

Biomes are terrestrial climax communities that have a wide geographic distribution. In general, the structure of ecosystems in a biome and the kinds of niches and habitats in those ecosystems are similar. However, it is important to recognize that although the concept of a biome is useful for discussing overall patterns and processes, different communities within a given type of biome show differences in the exact species present.

There are two major nonbiological factors that have an impact on the kind of community that develops in a given part of the world: precipitation pattern and temperature range. The aspects of precipitation that are most important are the total amount of precipitation per year, the form of precipitation (rain, snow, sleet), and its seasonal distribution. Temperature patterns vary greatly throughout regions of the world. Some regions, like tropical areas near the equator or areas near the poles, have a relatively consistent temperature throughout the year; other areas are more evenly divided between cold and warm temperatures. Each type of biome is dependent in large part on precipitation and temperature.

### Desert

Deserts are one type of biome in which there are generally less than 25 centimeters of precipitation per year. The form of precipitation varies for each desert. Although deserts are typically thought to be hot and dry (Sahara and the desert of the Southwestern United States), there are some desert biomes in which temperatures are quite cool for a major part of the year (Gobi Desert and the deserts of the Northwestern United States) or even bitterly cold (Dry Valleys of Antarctica).

Many species populate a desert biome, but there are usually a low number of individuals of each species. In the past, humans had little impact on desert biomes in part because the hot, arid conditions did not allow for agriculture. Hunter-gatherer societies were most common in deserts. However, modern technology allows for water to be transported into deserts, cities have developed in some desert biomes, and there is also limited agriculture.

## Grassland

Temperate grassland biomes such as prairies or steppes are widely distributed in temperate regions of Earth. Grasslands generally receive 25–75 centimeters of rain annually. In general, grassland biomes are windy with hot summers and cold winters. In many grassland biomes, fire is an important factor in releasing nutrients from dead plants into the soil and for preventing the invasion of trees. Between 60 and 90 percent of the vegetation is grass. Primary consumers eat the grasses, and there are often large herds of migratory animals such as bison living in grasslands. Carnivores also inhabit grasslands. Most of the moist grasslands throughout the world have been converted to agriculture. Drier grasslands have been converted to grazing for domestic grazers such as cattle, sheep, and goats. There is very little undisturbed grassland left.

## Savanna

Savannas are found in tropical parts of Africa, South America, and Australia. They are characterized by extensive grasslands and occasional patches of trees. These biomes typically have a rainy season in which 50 to 150 centimeters of rain fall, followed by a drought period. Plants and animals time their reproductive activities to coincide with the rainy season, when food and water are more abundant. Savannas have been heavily impacted by agriculture. Farming is possible in moister regions, and animal grazing is found in drier regions. Irrigation is essential because of the long periods of drought.

## Mediterranean Shrublands (Chaparral)

Mediterranean shrublands are located near oceans and are dominated by low shrubs. The climate varies from wet, cool winters to hot, dry summers. Rainfall is 40 to 100 centimeters per year. Vegetation is dominated by woody shrubs, and the types of animals vary widely. Very little shrubland exists that has not been impacted by humans. There are many major cities in this type of biome and also a large amount of agriculture.

## Tropical Dry Forest

Tropical dry forests are heavily influenced by seasonal rainfall. This type of biome is found in parts of Central and South America, Australia, Africa, and Asia. Many tropical dry forests have monsoon seasons, and rainfall ranges from 50 to 200 centimeters. There are generally high human populations in tropical dry forests, and wood is harvested from them for fuel and building materials.

## Tropical Rain Forest

Tropical rain forests are located near the equator in Central and South America, Africa, Southeast Asia, and some islands in the Caribbean Sea and Pacific Ocean. The temperature is warm and relatively constant, and it rains nearly every day, 200–500 centimeters a year. There is extensive vegetation, but soils are generally poor because all of the nutrients are taken up by plants. Tropical rain forests have a greater diversity of species than any other biome. Today, tropical rainforests are under intense pressure from logging and agricultural industries, although agriculture is generally not successful in the long term because of typically poor soil conditions.

## Temperate Deciduous Forest

Temperate deciduous forests have changes of seasons, and trees lose their leaves in fall and regrow leaves in spring. This forest is typical in the eastern half of the United States, parts of South Central and Southeastern Canada, Southern Africa, and many areas of Europe and Asia. Winters are generally mild, and plants actively grow for about six months. There are generally 75 to 100 centimeters of precipitation per year distributed evenly. Each region of the world has certain species of trees and other organisms. Most of the temperate deciduous forests have been heavily impacted by human activity. Much has been cleared for agriculture and logging and to develop major population areas.

## Taiga, Northern Coniferous Forest, or Boreal Forest

The evergreen coniferous forests found throughout Southern Canada, parts of Northern Europe, and Russia are known as taiga, northern coniferous forests, or boreal forests. These biomes have 30 to 85 centimeters of precipitation per year, and there is a great deal of snowmelt in spring contributing to humid climates. These regions have many lakes, ponds, and bogs, and conifers are the most common organisms in these biomes. Humans have a less severe impact on these biomes because of low population density. Logging and herding of reindeer are common activities.

## Tundra

Tundra is the area north of taiga biomes. It is an extremely cold region with permanently frozen subsoil (permafrost), which means tundra is mostly full of short grasses and there are no trees. Tundra biomes experience ten months of winter. Less than 25 centimeters of precipitation fall each year, but summer months see generally wet soil conditions due to snowmelt. Water is not absorbed into the soil because of the permafrost subsoil layer. Therefore, many shallow ponds and waterlogged areas exist in summer. Also in summer months, there is a variety of small plants and swarms of insects that are a food source for migratory birds and waterfowl. Tundra is also home to a few hardy mammals such as reindeer and arctic hare. Many species of birds and large mammals migrate during summer months using the scattered patches of small communities known as alpine tundra. Very few people live in tundra biomes, but any damage to this ecosystem is slow to heal because of the very short growing season. Tundra land must be handled with care.

## Aquatic Ecosystems

Aquatic ecosystems are shaped by the ability of the sun's energy to penetrate the water, the depth of the water, the nature of the bottom of the body of water, the water temperature, and the amount of salts dissolved in the water. Freshwater ecosystems have little dissolved salt, and marine ecosystems have a high salt content.

Oceans are defined as pelagic marine ecosystems and have many organisms that float or actively swim. **Plankton** are very small, sometimes microscopic organisms that are found in large numbers in oceans and large lakes and are an important food source for larger animals. **Zooplankton** are small animals (including larvae of larger organisms), while **phytoplankton** are microscopic plants or plant-like organisms that carry out photosynthesis. Phytoplankton, such as algae, live in the euphotic zone, the upper layers of the ocean where the sun's rays penetrate. The open ocean in the euphotic zone is known as the pelagic zone; closer to the coast, above the continental shelf is the neritic zone.

- **Benthic Marine Ecosystems:** Organisms that live on the bottom of oceans are part of benthic marine ecosystems (benthic systems are called littoral in shallow water near the coast). The substrate material on the ocean bottom is important in determining which species live in a particular benthic ecosystem. Temperature also has an impact on benthic ecosystems. An abyssal ecosystem is a benthic ecosystem that is situated in great depths of the ocean. No light reaches these ecosystems, so animals must depend on the fall of organic matter from the euphotic zone.

- **Coral Reef Ecosystems:** These are produced by coral animals that build up around themselves cup-shaped external skeletons. The skeletons of corals provide a surface upon which many other species live. Coral reef systems require warm water and are, therefore, found only near the equator.

- **Mangrove Swamp Ecosystems:** These are tropical forest ecosystems found in shallow waters near the shore of marine ecosystems and an adjacent landmass. These ecosystems are dominated by trees that can tolerate the high salt content of the water and excrete salt from their leaves. Seeds of these trees germinate on the tree itself, and then fall into the water and are buried in mud where they take root. These trees have extensive root systems that extend above water to take in oxygen. Mangroves are found in Southern Florida, the Caribbean, Southeast Asia, and Africa, as well as many other tropical and subtropical coasts.

- **Estuary Ecosystems:** An estuary is an ecosystem consisting of shallow water and a partially enclosed area where fresh water runs into the ocean. The salt content of water in estuaries changes with the tide and the inflow and outflow of the rivers. Organisms in this type of ecosystem have adapted to these changing conditions. An estuary is a productive ecosystem because the shallow regions allow light to penetrate the water, and rich nutrients are dumped from rivers into the basin of an estuary.

- **Freshwater Ecosystems:** These have a much lower salt content than marine ecosystems and have a large range of water temperature. Freshwater ecosystems consist of either relatively stationary water, such as lakes, ponds, or reservoirs, or moving water, such as streams or rivers. If a lake is deep enough, it has similar characteristics to an ocean ecosystem: There is a euphotic zone at the top, and there are many kinds of phytoplankton and zooplankton. Emergent plants grow near the shores and shallower regions of lakes. They are rooted to the bottom of the lakes and their leaves can float on the surface (water lily) or stick out above the water's surface (cattail). Submerged plants are rooted below the surface, but do not protrude above the surface (*Elodea* and *Chara*). The region of a lake with rooted vegetation is called the littoral zone, and the region where vegetation is not rooted is called the limnetic zone.

The productivity of a lake is dependent upon water temperature and depth. **Oligotrophic lakes** are deep, clear, cold and have a low nutrient content. There is low productivity in this type of lake. On the other hand, **eutrophic lakes** are shallow, murky, warm, and nutrient-rich. Productivity is higher in these lakes.

The dissolved oxygen content of water is also important to ecosystems. It determines the kind of organisms that inhabit a lake. When organic molecules enter water, bacteria and fungi break them down. The amount of oxygen used by these decomposers to break down a specific amount of organic matter is known as the **biochemical oxygen demand (BOD)**.

In streams and rivers, water is moving, so organisms like algae attach to rocks. The collection of algae and fungi in streams and rivers is called periphyton. Most streams are shallow, and light can penetrate to the bottom, but because the water is fast-moving, photosynthetic organisms do not accumulate enough essential nutrients for growth. Therefore, most streams are not very productive.

Most of the nutrients come from organic matter that falls into streams. In rivers, the water is deeper, and there is less light penetration. Organisms must rely on nutrients flowing in from streams. Rivers tend to be larger than streams with warmer, slower-moving water. Therefore, there is less oxygen in rivers, and frequently different species occupy rivers and streams.

Swamps and marshes delineate the transition from terrestrial ecosystems into freshwater aquatic ecosystems. Swamps are wetlands that contain trees that withstand the flooded conditions. Marshes are wetlands dominated by grasses and reeds.

Most freshwater ecosystems have been heavily impacted by human activity. Activity on land affects freshwater systems because there is runoff from land into lakes, rivers, and streams. Agricultural runoff, sewage, and trash affect freshwater ecosystems. Human impact on marine ecosystems comes in the form of overfishing, oil pollution from transportation, oil spills, and trash dumping.

## Population Biology

Population biology is a branch of environmental science that is concerned with characterizing the make-up and growth of populations and their impact on the environment and its organisms. A population is a group of individuals of one species that inhabits a given area. Population dynamics focus on the growth and limitations of a population and how that population interacts with its environment with respect to its growth and stability. Population genetics addresses the frequency and distribution of specific genes in a population and how these frequencies might change over time. Population genetics is also concerned with mutation rates within a given population. Different populations of the same species have different characteristics such as birthrate, mortality, sex ratio, age distribution, growth rate, migration rate, spatial distribution, and density. Demography describes the vital statistics of a given population.

**Birthrate:** The number of individuals added to a population over a particular time period, through reproduction of the species. Asexual reproduction is the process in which an organism such as bacteria divides to form new individuals. Sexual reproduction is the most common type of reproduction. Most species produce many more offspring than are needed to replace the parent generation. The birthrate in humans is usually described as the number of offspring produced by 1,000 individuals in a given year.

**Death Rate or Mortality Rate:** The number of deaths in a population over a given time period. For most species, mortality rates are high, but in humans it is relatively low. One way to study mortality is with a survivorship curve, which shows the proportion of individuals likely to survive at each age. The death rate in humans is referred to as the number of people in 1,000 that die per year. For a population to grow, the birthrate must exceed the death rate in a given year.

**Sex Ratio:** The relative number of males and females in a given population. The number of females has a bigger effect on the number of offspring produced in a population. However, the typical ratio approximates 1:1.

**Age Distribution:** The number of individuals in each age range in a population. Age distribution has a large influence on population growth rates. Among humans, different societies see vastly different age distributions. In general, a large reproductive population will cause future population growth.

**Population Density:** The number of organisms within a species in a given area. Movement from a densely populated region is called **dispersal**. Dispersal relieves overcrowding in a given area. The migration of individuals is referred to as **emigration**. Some organisms may leave their population to become members of a different population. This is called **migration**, or **immigration**. Biological ability to produce offspring is a species' biotic potential. Because most species have a high biotic potential, there is a natural tendency for populations to increase. In general, there is an exponential growth in populations for a given period. There is often a pattern of growth that includes the following:

- A lag phase in which the population grows more slowly
- An exponential growth phase
- A declaration phase in which population growth slows due to equal birth and death rates, which leads to
- A stabile equilibrium phase in which there is a stable population size

There are several main environmental factors that limit population size. Factors from outside a population are known as **extrinsic limiting factors**. Factors regulated within a population are called **intrinsic limiting factors**. As the population increases, density-dependent limiting factors are important. **Density-independent limiting factors** are influences that control population, but they are not dependent on limiting factors. Limiting factors can be divided into four main categories:

1. Availability of raw materials
2. Availability of energy
3. Accumulation of waste products
4. Interaction between organisms

The **carrying capacity** is the maximum population that can be sustained in a given area. The carrying capacity is determined by a set of limiting factors. Environmental changes such as forest fires or floods can change the carrying capacity of an area.

A given species has a particular reproduction strategy.

- **K -strategists** are organisms that tend to reach a stable population as the carrying capacity is reached. These species tend to occupy a stable environment and tend to be large organisms that have a long lifespan, produce few offspring, and expend a lot of energy to care for their offspring. These populations tend to be limited by density-dependent limiting factors.
- **R-strategists** tend to be small organisms that have a short lifespan, produce many offspring, do not reach the carrying capacity, and live in unstable environments. These organisms produce many offspring, but do not expend energy to care for them. These species tend to be limited by density-independent limiting factors.

In northern regions of the world, many species follow a population cycle in which periods of large populations are followed by periods of small populations. In general, this occurs because of the nature of ecosystems in this part of the world. Ecosystems are relatively simple with few organisms affecting one another.

## Natural Selection and Evolution

Natural selection is the process that determines which individuals within a species will survive and reproduce, thereby passing their genes on to the next generation. Changes observed over time in the physical appearance or behavior of a species are due to the process of evolution. Individuals in a species who are best adapted to a certain environment will survive best and produce more offspring, thus changing the characteristics of a given species over a long period of time. Therefore, natural selection is the mechanism that causes the evolution of a species.

There are several factors involved in the process of natural selection. Individuals within a species have genetic variation; some of the variations are useful, and some are not. Organisms reproduce at such a rate that many more offspring are produced than are needed to replace the parent generation, but most of the offspring die. The excess number of offspring results in a shortage of food supplies and other resources.

However, because there is a genetic variation among individuals of a species, some have a greater chance of obtaining the necessary food and resources (or avoiding danger) and, therefore, are more likely to survive and reproduce. Over time, each generation is subjected to the same process of natural selection, so that the percentage of individuals with favorable variations will increase, and the number of individuals with unfavorable variations will decrease.

Therefore, over time, there is a considerable change in the type of species present and their characteristics. Some changes can take place in a few generations, whereas others have taken thousands or millions of years. The process of natural selection plays a key role in evolution, and through the study of fossil records, it is obvious to see that some new species evolve, while others die out.

- **Speciation** is the development of a new species from a previously existing species. In general, speciation occurs as two subpopulations adapt to different conditions and eventually are unable to interbreed because they are so different.
- **Polyploidy** is a condition in plants in which there is an increase in the number of chromosomes in the cells, and this can also lead to the development of a new species that cannot interbreed with the original species.

- **Extinction** is the loss of an entire species and is a common feature in evolutionary history. In general, extinction comes about due to changes in a species' environment or from human intervention.
- **Coevolution** is the idea that two or more species of organisms can influence the evolutionary path of the other. This is a common pattern since all organisms within an ecosystem influence one another.

## Succession

Ecosystems respond to environmental challenges through succession. Succession is a series of recognizable and predictable changes over time to maintain the stability of the community. Succession occurs because the activities of a given species cause changes to the environment that make it suitable for other species. Succession proceeds until a stable climax community is reached.

There are two general types of succession:

1. **Primary succession** in new life is colonized in an environment that has a complete lack of life form and minimal water. Primary succession can occur in areas where volcanic activity wipes out life forms in an ecosystem. Primary succession takes a very long time to establish.
2. **Secondary succession** occurs when a portion of an ecosystem is disturbed by an event such as a forest fire. In this case, the area is eventually restored through succession, and it is a much more rapid process than primary succession because soil and water are usually already present.

Regardless of whether succession is primary or secondary, the process occurs in basically the same manner. First, new land is exposed. This land is either devoid of life (primary succession) or disturbed in some way (secondary succession). Next, pioneer species take root. Pioneer species are generally fast-growing plants that can thrive in exposed conditions and have a short lifespan.

Usually, lichen (an organism that includes both fungus and algae in a symbiotic relationship) or mosses begin to modify the ecosystem for the growth of other species. The collection of organisms at this stage is known as the **pioneer community**. Eventually, as a thin layer of soil is established, longer-lived plants are established. Each step in the sequence from the pioneer community to the climax community is a **successional**, or **seral stage**. The entire sequence of stages is known as a sere. At each seral stage, species either replace or coexist with previously existing species, and the ecosystem continues to be further modified at each stage, until the climax community is attained.

In a **climax community**, longer-living plants and animals are sustained by the environment. The difference between a climax community and a successional (seral) community is that climax communities maintain their diversity of species for a long time, and successional communities are temporary.

The organisms in a climax community maintain specialized niches, recycle nutrients, and maintain a relatively constant biomass, whereas successional communities do not. The general trend in succession is toward increasing complexity and efficiency.

With respect to aquatic ecosystems, with the exception of the oceans, most aquatic ecosystems are temporary. All aquatic systems receive a continuous input of soil and organic matter, and eventually bodies of water are filled in. This may take thousands of years, but it is a continual process. The successional stages of aquatic ecosystems are often called "wet meadow" stages and mark the transition of an aquatic community to a terrestrial community.

# ENVIRONMENTAL IMPACTS

Approximately 25 percent of the questions on the DSST Environmental Science exam will cover topics dealing with environmental impacts. Let's review all the major concepts you will need to know for the exam.

## Human Population Dynamics

Human population has been steadily increasing since the modern era, mostly because of the longer life span of populations. Developed countries have an increase in food production and better methods of controlling disease. All of this can be shared with the rest of the world, resulting in an improved quality of life overall. The world population is currently increasing at a rate of 1.12 percent annually, a slight decline from a decade ago.

At this rate, the world population is expected to reach 9.6 billion in 2050. Several factors must be taken into consideration to fully understand human population growth. Economic development plays a huge role in population growth; birthrates tend to be higher in developing countries, a combination of low childhood survival and lower access to family planning. More developed countries usually, have a relatively stable population growth, and less-developed countries do not.

Several factors interact to determine the impact of a society's population growth on the resources of a country. These factors include the following:

- Land
- Natural resources
- Size of a population
- Quantity of natural resources consumed
- Environmental damage caused by using resources

The relationship of all these factors can be expressed in the equation:

**Impact on the Environment =**

**Population × Affluence × Damage Due to Technology**

**or (I = P × A × T)**

Population density relates the size of a population to available resources. People in highly developed countries tend to have a greater impact on the environment because of technological development.

The **ecological footprint** of a population is a measure of the land and resources required to support the population and absorb its waste.

**Demography** is the study of human populations, their characteristics, and the consequences of growth. Demographers can predict future population growth by looking at biological factors, including the total fertility rate and age distribution. The total fertility rate is the average number of children a woman will bear in her lifetime. A total fertility rate of 2.1 is a replacement fertility rate whereby parents will be replaced by offspring when they die. If the number of births equals the number of deaths, there is zero population growth. Social factors that influence population growth are aspects like culture, traditions, and attitudes towards birth control. Women's rights have been determined to be a major factor; when women gain more influence over reproductive and economic decisions, birth rates tend to fall.

Political factors also influence human population growth. In many advanced economies such as Italy and Japan, the population is actually declining as birthrates have dropped below replacement level. As a result, some developed countries try to promote more births, whereas countries like China facing overpopulation have taken measures to control growth. Immigration also has an impact on the rate of growth in a population.

A human population often increases only if populations of other animals and plants decrease. When humans need food, they convert ecosystems into agricultural systems. In some cases, the long-term health of the environment is sacrificed to feed a population. Countries with the highest standard of living seem to have the lowest rate of population growth, and those with the lowest standard of living have the highest population growth rate.

This leads to the demographic transition model that occurs in four stages.

1. Initially, countries have a stable population with a high birthrate and death rate.
2. Improved economic and social conditions cause a decrease in the death rate, so there is a period of rapid population growth.
3. As countries develop an industrial economy, birthrates drop and population growth rates fall.
4. Eventually, birthrates and death rates are balanced again, but this time there is a low birthrate and low death rate.

## Global Climate Change

The atmosphere is composed of 78.1 percent nitrogen, 20.9 percent oxygen, and 1 percent of a mixture of other gases, including carbon dioxide, methane, and water vapor. The atmosphere is composed of four layers: from the surface up to the edge of space they are troposphere, stratosphere, mesosphere, and the thermosphere.

Energy from the sun enters the atmosphere, but not all of that energy reaches Earth's surface. Clouds and gases high in the atmosphere reflect back about 25 percent of the sun's energy. Denser gas absorbs more energy, and gases are densest in the troposphere. Another 25 percent are absorbed by gases in the atmosphere, such as ozone, carbon dioxide, methane, and water vapor. These gases are known as greenhouse gases (GHGs). Of the 50 percent of the energy that reaches Earth's surface, some is reflected back into the atmosphere by rain, snow, ice, and sand. The rest is absorbed by Earth's surface.

The greenhouse effect is natural, and without our atmosphere to trap heat from the sun, Earth would not be warm enough to sustain life. However, since the Industrial Revolution (discussed later in this chapter), human activities have added extra greenhouse gases into the atmosphere. Major human sources of greenhouse gases include burning of fossil fuels for industrial processes, power generation, and transportation; clearing and burning of forests;, and methane from livestock. There are natural sources of greenhouse gases as well, such as respiration and volcanic activity. The increased concentration of GHGs in the atmosphere increases the percentage of the sun's energy that is trapped by the atmosphere.

In 1898, Swedish scientist Svante Arrhenius calculated how much surface temperature might increase if atmospheric carbon dioxide increased. His work was built upon by Charles Keeling, whose work first linked increased anthropogenic carbon dioxide to observed temperature increases. So far, the average surface temperature has increased about 2° Fahrenheit since the 19th century, and human activities are believed to be responsible for most of that increase. There is a range of predictions about how much the global average temperature will continue to increase, depending on what actions are taken, and due to natural processes. The Intergovernmental Panel on Climate Change (IPCC) is tasked with processing the available data on climate change and producing regular reports on the subject.

The oceans have absorbed a large portion of excess $CO_2$ and heat, so ocean temperatures have increased and water chemistry is at risk of changing. The increased carbon dioxide forms a weak acid when mixed with seawater, a process called **ocean acidification**. Acidification may hinder marine organisms, such as coral, from properly forming shells or skeletons.

The possible outcomes of a global temperature increase, some of which have already been observed, will vary across the planet and will not be felt equally. Most of the hottest years have occurred since the year 2000, but not every single place on Earth has experienced record high temperatures. It is for this reason that the term global climate change is used instead of global warming; local weather continues to be highly variable.

At the moment, the greatest impacts are in the polar regions, where ice caps and sea ice cover have shrunk considerably. Glaciers at lower latitudes have also retreated. (Less ice means that less heat is reflected back into space, increasing the rate of change.) Some areas may see increased rainfall, while others may experience drought. Longer and more intense heat waves are likely, as are more intense storms. Species have begun to move around in search of their preferred temperature range; species that cannot easily move to cooler areas, particularly mountain species, are at risk of extinction. It is difficult to predict the exact timescale for these changes or to say exactly what will happen in any particular place.

Most researchers believe these changes to be inevitable unless either GHG emissions are drastically reduced or a way is found to remove excess GHGs from the atmosphere.

# Pollution

Pollution is any matter or energy that has harmful effects when introduced into the environment. Pollution can enter the environment naturally, for example through a volcanic eruption, but humans are most often the source.

## Physical Aspects of Pollution

Pollution can take almost any physical form—for example, solid waste like your household trash—but pollution can also be liquid or gas. Chemical pollution can settle into soil and remain there, forever unless the soil is decontaminated or excavated.

Pollution, generally gas or very small particles, that enters the air is called air pollution. Sources of outdoor air pollution include industrial output (smokestacks), engine emissions, power generation, accidental release from fossil fuel extraction, and fires, among others. Physical or atmospheric features, such as mountains or temperature inversions, can trap air pollution close to the ground, especially in populated areas. Indoor sources of air pollution may include cigarette smoke or radon, a naturally occurring radioactive gas.

Pollution that enters surface or ground water is water pollution. Water pollution is the result of population growth and industrial growth. A source of water pollution that is readily identifiable because it has a definite point where it enters the water is called a point source. Diffuse pollutants such as those that come from agricultural runoff, urban roadways, and rain are nonpoint sources of water pollution. Types of water pollution include municipal, agricultural, industrial, thermal, marine oil, and groundwater pollution.

## Chemical Aspects of Pollution

There are several categories of air pollutants on Earth.

1. Primary air pollutants are released into the atmosphere in unmodified forms. These pollutants include carbon monoxide, volatile organic compounds (hydrocarbons), particulate matter, sulfur dioxide, and oxides of nitrogen.
2. Secondary air pollutants are primary pollutants that can interact with other compounds in the presence of sunlight to form new compounds such as ozone. **Photochemical smog**, a word formed by *smoke* and *fog*, is a secondary pollutant formed when emissions combine and react in the atmosphere to form a dense, low-lying layer of air pollution.

3. The U.S. Environmental Protection Agency (EPA) has a category of air pollutants called criteria air pollutants. These include nitrogen dioxide, ozone, sulfur dioxide, particulate matter, carbon monoxide, and lead.

## Ozone

Ozone is a molecule that consists of three oxygen atoms bound to one another. Ground-level ozone is an extremely reactive molecule that can cause irritation to respiratory tissue and damage to lungs.

Ozone is a secondary pollutant formed as a component of photochemical smog. However, there is also a necessary layer of ozone (the ozone layer) in the atmosphere that shields Earth from the harmful effects of ultraviolet (UV) radiation from the sun. This ozone layer is slowly being depleted as a result of pollutants, especially chlorofluorocarbons (CFC), in the atmosphere. Less ozone in the upper atmosphere results in more UV light reaching Earth's surface. This can lead to increased risks of skin cancer, cataracts, and mutations.

The combination of sulfur dioxide or oxides of nitrogen with an oxidizing agent like ozone, hydroxide ions, or hydrogen peroxide, along with water, forms sulfuric and nitric acid in the atmosphere. Acid-forming particles are dissolved in rain, sleet, snow, and fog and can also be deposited as dry particles. All forms of precipitation that contain acid-forming particles are known as **acid rain**. The accumulation of acid-forming particles on a surface is known as acid deposition. Acid rain is a worldwide problem that stems from natural causes, such as vegetation, volcanoes, and lightning, as well as human activities, including burning of fossil fuels and the use of the internal combustion engine.

Water pollution can take many forms. Common water pollutants include oil or salt washed from road surfaces, pesticides, discarded medications, detergent, or raw sewage. One important category of water pollutants is the oxygen binders, substances that can remove oxygen from water. Ethylene glycol—antifreeze—has this property.

Agricultural runoff (e.g., fertilizer or animal waste) is another major source of water pollution. The excess nutrients, when washed into a body of water, promote high algae and plant growth. Eutrophication can result, or the surplus algae begins to die. Decomposition uses up the oxygen in the water. These oxygen-free areas are known as "dead zones." A large dead zone forms every year in the Gulf of Mexico near the mouth of the Mississippi River, caused by agricultural runoff washing out with the river.

## Biological Aspects of Pollution

Pollution may have a variety of biological impacts. Acid rain, for example, is suspected of causing the death of many forests, and it also causes damage to human-made structures, especially those made of limestone. Sulfuric acid converts limestone to gypsum, which then erodes away. There are also effects of acid rain on aquatic ecosystems, as evidenced in a progressive loss of organisms as the acidity of the water increases.

Some pollutants may be directly toxic to life; different substances are tested to determine the maximum allowable concentration in water before harm occurs to aquatic life. For pollutants that do not break down but linger in the environment, **biomagnification** or **bioaccumulation** is a problem. Small organisms consume small amounts of a pollutant; larger organisms eat many smaller organisms and accumulate all of the pollutants consumed by each of those small organisms. For example, higher and higher trophic levels feed on lower-level organisms, so the concentration of a pollutant accumulates and can be up to 2,000 times the original concentration in the highest trophic-level species.

Air pollution can settle into the ground or water, impacting soil or water chemistry, and impacting terrestrial and aquatic life. All forms of pollution can have health impacts on humans, but air pollution in particular is linked to numerous health concerns, including heart and respiratory disease. Children chronically exposed to air pollution are particularly at risk.

## Agricultural Impacts of Pollution

Early civilizations obtained food by hunting and gathering. The development of agriculture required domestication of wild plants into a controlled setting and greater control over land and soil. Food plants were manipulated through selective breeding to produce crops with greater nutrition and better taste (e.g., potatoes). Land had to be cleared to make way for crops and pastures for livestock.

The increase in yield of food grown allowed for an increase in populations (an increase in K for humans). With the advent of the Industrial Revolution, agriculture was also mechanized.

To operate effectively, new machines required large tracts of relatively flat land planted with a single crop, a practice known as **monoculture**. Although these methods produce abundant crops of food, the clearing of large tracts of land also leads to soil erosion and soil depleted of nutrients, which must be added back to the soil. Because of erosion problems, many farmers now use methods that reduce the time a field is left fallow.

Domestication of livestock has its own environmental concerns. Erosion also results from clearing forests to create space for animals, and overgrazing can damage fragile grasslands and ranges. A lot of viable land is required to grow feed for livestock, land that can't be used for other purposes.

## Industrial Impacts of Pollution

The Industrial Revolution, beginning in the mid-1700s, was brought about by the use of coal as a major fuel source in England. It involved the invention of the steam engine and the development of machines to mass-produce goods. The steam engine also made large-scale coal mining possible. During the Industrial Revolution and afterwards, energy consumption increased, economies grew, and populations became more prosperous. An increase in coal use also caused an increase in air pollution, including a rapid increase in atmospheric $CO_2$ levels. Within the span of 200 years, energy consumption increased eightfold, and pollution became a serious problem in some countries. Industrialization made manufacturing much easier and cheaper, leading to a rise in disposable products (e.g., plastic bottles). Cheap, disposable manufactured goods led to a higher level of consumption, especially in wealthier nations, as well as increased resource use. The young science of industrial ecology, which aims to limit ecological impacts of industrial processes, may mitigate some of these environmental concerns.

Currently, the most rapid industrial development takes place in emerging nations. This development leads to a disproportionate amount of ecosystem degradation and loss of biodiversity in those countries. The damage to the environment in these nations can actually increase poverty instead of promoting wealth. Some economists believe that the ecological damage levels off when developing economies reach a suitable level of development.

## Habitat Destruction

To clear land for agriculture, farmers clear large tracts of forestland, a process called **deforestation**. Deforestation is mainly used for agricultural purposes, or to make room for human settlement. In some countries, forests are still cleared for wood to be used as a fuel source or for building materials. Even when only some of the trees are removed a forest can suffer damage. Removal of trees in tropical regions removes biomass, which contains most of the nutrients in the soil. The soil that is left is poor and not ideal for agriculture. In addition, deforestation leads to erosion of soil.

Deforestation causes carbon dioxide to stay in the atmosphere because there are fewer trees to take it in, which contributes to global warming. Evapotranspiration through the leaves of trees returns water to the atmosphere as part of the hydrologic cycle, but deforestation reduces this process and disrupts the hydrologic cycle. Deforestation also disrupts ecosystems and species that live in forests.

Patchwork clear-cutting, reforestation, and selective harvesting are methods used to try to avoid deforestation. When forests are left alone, they will grow back, but never to the same original state.

Habitats can also be destroyed in other ways. Waste disposal, especially improper disposal, can leave soil and land contaminated and even virtually destroyed. Excess use of motorized vehicles or even too much foot traffic can disrupt fragile landscapes, especially in desert or alpine systems. Wetlands and marshes can be dredged away to make room for shipping or they can be filled in, either to dispose of material or to make more room for development. Even something as small as mowing an old field can destroy natural habitat.

Mining, for fossil fuels or ore, also takes a toll on the environment.

- Coal or metals can be extracted by surface, or strip, mining, which involves removing the overburden material on top of a vein of coal to get to the coal below the surface. This method is efficient, but it disrupts the landscape. In the United States, regulations require that retired surface mines be replanted with vegetation, but habitat is rarely restored to its original condition.
- Underground mining extracts coal that is buried deep beneath Earth's surface. The method poses many safety concerns and health hazards for miners, but it doesn't disturb the aboveground landscape. However, underground mining still raises environmental issues such as subsidence, or sinking of the land, and the accumulation of large waste heaps. Mine waste, known as tailings, often contains toxic chemicals and disposal can cause extensive habitat damage, especially when sediment or toxins run into streams.

Marine habitats can be destroyed by illegal fishing techniques such as fishing with explosives, or damaged by legal but destructive techniques such as bottom trawling.

The excessive growth of algae and other aquatic plants in water with added nutrients is a process called **eutrophication**. When phosphates or nitrates are added to the surface of a body of water from sources such as organic waste from agriculture or industries, they can act as a fertilizer and cause excessive growth of algae. This undesirable algae growth can interfere with the use of the water. Also, as the algae dies, there is a decrease in oxygen levels in the water, and fish and other aquatic life die.

## Land Degradation

Land, especially farm and rangeland, is a finite resource that can be lost if not properly cared for. Farmland is at risk of erosion; without the plants to hold the soil in place, soil can blow or wash away between crops under many farming methods. The nutrients in the soil can be used up if too many of the same crops (monoculture) are planted for too many years, without rotating in different crops to replenish the soil. Continuous farming, particularly monocultures, can eventually leave the soil unsuitable for farming.

Rangelands are vulnerable to overgrazing, especially in times of drought. Cattle and other livestock are often grazed in arid and semi-arid landscapes. If too many animals are allowed to feed before the plants can regrow, then erosion and fire risk increase. This problem is especially acute on publicly owned lands.

The conversion of dry, arid, or semiarid land into desert-like ecosystems is a process called **desertification**. Desertification is most prevalent in Northern Africa and parts of Asia where there is irregular or unpredictable rainfall. In many of these areas, there are populations of nomadic herders or subsistence farmers that are under pressure to provide food for their families, even at a cost to the environment. Overgrazing and over-farming lead to desertification in these areas.

## ENVIRONMENTAL MANAGEMENT AND CONSERVATION

Environmental management and conservation involves a number of highly contentious political issues. Approximately 25 percent of the questions on the DSST Environmental Science exam will cover topics dealing with this topic.

## Nonrenewable Resources

Natural resources are those that humans can use for their own purposes, but that they cannot create. Soil, wind, and water are all examples of natural resources. A renewable resource can be formed or regenerated by natural processes, so that it is not used up. However, nonrenewable resources are not replaced by natural processes. Fossil fuels and mountain ranges are nonrenewable on a human timescale.

The energy sources most commonly used by industrialized nations are fossil fuels: oil, coal, and natural gas. They constitute 87 percent of the world's energy sources and are all nonrenewable resources, but that number is expected to decrease slowly. Humans are using up nonrenewable energy sources at a much faster rate than they can be replaced, which eventually will exhaust Earth's supply of these sources.

Coal mining and coal transport generates a lot of dust in the atmosphere, and there is also sulfur associated with coal that causes acid mine drainage and air pollution. Burning of coal causes acid deposition in the atmosphere, which is a cause of acid rain. The release of carbon dioxide from coal has become a greater concern with respect to the potential for global warming. Burning oil produces fewer emissions than coal but is still a major source of greenhouse gases and there are major problems associated with spills and leaks from oil pipelines.

In recent years, natural gas has become a greater source of energy for electricity production and heat, especially in the United States. As of 2017, natural gas was cheaper than oil, and produces fewer emissions when burned. However, methane leaking from wells, refineries, storage, and transportation of natural gas are serious concerns since methane is a potent greenhouse gas. A controversial method of extracting gas (and oil) called **hydraulic fracturing**, involves splitting open shale rock with water and chemicals, creating issues of wastewater disposal and air pollution from machinery. The practice has led to lower fuel prices but has also been banned in some countries and U.S. states.

## Renewable Resources

As of 2015, only 13 percent of the world's power generation comes from non–fossil fuels. Of that, approximately 7 percent is from hydroelectric power, 4 percent is nuclear, and only 2 percent is from a combination of biomass, geothermal, wind, and solar energy.

- **Biomass** is used most in developing countries. All biomass is produced by green plants that convert sunlight into plant material through photosynthesis. Major types of biomass include wood, municipal and industrial wastes, agricultural crop residue, animal waste, and energy plantations. Plants such as sugar cane or corn may also be used to produce ethanol, an alternative fuel. The practice is controversial as it can drive up food prices. Using biomass fuels can create air pollution.

- **Hydroelectric power** relies on water to generate electricity. The construction of reservoirs, however, can cause environmental and social issues. One possible impact is that dams can cause flooding of land around them. Damming a river alters the natural flow and level of water in a river, and can impede the passage of migratory fish.

- **Tidal power** can also supply a renewable energy source, but this might result in negative impacts on shorelines. Currently, tidal generators are very costly.

- **Geothermal power** is linked to geologically active regions where thermal energy from Earth can reach the surface through thin layers of Earth's crust. Geothermal energy creates steam that contains hydrogen sulfide, which causes air pollution.

- **Wind power** is another source of energy, but it is dependent on the variability of winds. Places such as the Dakotas in the United States have the strongest winds, but because they are remote from large, energy-using population centers, there would be a loss in electricity if transferred to distant areas of the country. The moving blades of wind generators can pose a hazard to birds, depending on where the turbines are located. They can also produce noise that bothers nearby residents. More selective placement of wind farms and new technologies under development such as blade-free turbines may mitigate some of these concerns.

- **Solar energy** is a renewable energy source that can be collected through means of passive solar or active solar systems, but large solar farms can displace sensitive desert habitat.

- **Nuclear power** is generated when the heat from a controlled nuclear fission reaction is used to heat water and create steam, which is used to turn a turbine. Nuclear power produces very few emissions besides water vapor, but uranium fuel is a finite resource. The used fuel is highly toxic waste that is difficult to properly dispose, and nuclear accidents are rare but can be very serious. As a result, nuclear power has both renewable and non-renewable elements. Nuclear power remains controversial as an energy source.

## Agricultural Practices

The Green Revolution brought about the introduction of new varieties of plants and farming methods in the 1950s, '60s, and '70s. Both developed and developing countries benefited from the Green Revolution, and it has caused a significant increase in food production. The Green Revolution came about as a cooperative venture between Western countries to increase productivity and relieve hunger in Mexico and India. High-yield varieties of wheat were developed that were more resistant to pests and diseases. These new crops along with irrigation techniques and chemicals (fertilizers, pesticides, and herbicides) increased food production; however, many farmers in Mexico and India still remained poor.

Over time, more high-yield crops such as rice, sorghum, corn, and beans were introduced. Intensive farming methods to relieve hunger in Latin America and Asia were created. The Green Revolution has not been successful in parts of the world where the climate is arid and irrigation is not possible, such as sub-Saharan Africa. The Green Revolution also made crops more dependent on chemicals, which caused environmental concerns. The crop yield has increased as a result of the Green Revolution, but it has not solved the problems of world hunger.

The basic unit of agriculture is the farm, where farmers must clear land, plant seed, grow crops, and harvest them. Resources like land, water, soil, and seeds must be managed and conserved. There are several different types of agricultural methods practiced throughout the world.

- **Shifting agriculture** is practiced in many areas of the world where soil conditions are poor and human populations are low. It involves the cutting down and burning of trees in small area forests. Once the nutrients in the soil are depleted, the site is abandoned. In some parts of the world with poor soil conditions, such as tropical forests, this method is still used successfully.
- **Labor-intensive agriculture** is practiced in areas of the world with better soil conditions. It is still practiced in much of the world today, and it involves the extensive use of manual labor. This allows for low use of fossil fuels, but a lot of effort goes into an uncertain crop yield. In developing countries, the cost of manual labor is low compared to the cost of mechanized farming equipment.
- **Mechanized agriculture** developed after the beginning of the Industrial Revolution. This type of farming requires large tracts of mostly level land so the machines can operate, and the same crop is planted in large areas to maximize efficiency. In this type of farming, machines and fossil fuels have replaced human labor.

Fertilizers are used to increase crop yields. They can be valuable because they replace nutrients in the soil that are removed by plants. Macronutrients are the three primary soil nutrients: nitrogen, phosphorus, and potassium. Other micronutrients are also present in fertilizers (zinc, boron, manganese). Chemical fertilizers replace inorganic nutrients, but not organic materials in soil. The decomposition of organic matter returns organic nutrients to the soil.

Alternative agriculture methods include sustainable agriculture, which does not deplete soil, water wildlife, or human resources; organic agriculture, which prohibits the use of some pesticides and fertilizers; and other alternative agriculture practices that include all nontraditional methods such as hydroponics. Modern, more efficient irrigation methods such as trickle or drip irrigation, help conserve water by minimizing evaporation.

Precision agriculture is a technique of farming that addresses the concerns of conventional agricultural practices, such as fertilizer runoff in water supplies, pesticides accumulating in food chains, and groundwater contaminated by fertilizers. Computer technology allows farmers to vary the amount of fertilizers applied to different places in a crop. Thus, farmers use less chemicals overall more effectively.

## Pesticides and Pest Control

In addition to fertilizers, modern mechanized farming practices require other chemicals such as pesticides, insecticides, fungicides, denticides, and herbicides. These chemicals can cause damage to the environment and many species. The use of persistent pesticides, such as DDT or toxaphene, has been mostly banned because of hazardous impacts on wildlife. These pesticides do not break down in the environment and remain a threat to food chains for many years. Non-persistent pesticides such as organophosphates break down fairly rapidly. Pesticides often end up in nearby water supplies where they can be hazardous to aquatic life.

Another problem with pesticides is that pest populations such as insects, weeds, rodents, and fungi can become resistant to the chemicals. Over 500 species of insects have developed resistance to pesticides. Most pesticides are not specific to a particular organism and end up killing beneficial species as well as harmful ones.

There are also health concerns to humans who either apply pesticides or ingest foods with pesticide residues. For most people, the most critical health problems are related to exposure to small quantities over a long period of time. Many pesticides cause mutations, cancer, and abnormal offspring in experimental animals. Despite this, pesticide use in many countries continues to increase because more food can be produced with the use of pesticides, fewer crops are lost to pests, and less money is lost by farmers.

A controversial modern method of pest control is genetic modification, where certain plants have been genetically altered to deter insects on their own. In many cases, such modifications have significantly reduced the use of insecticides. The effect of genetic modifications to reduce the need for herbicides have had less obvious results. Many consumers reject genetically modified organisms (GMOs) and some countries require products containing GMOs to be specially labeled.

## Soil Conservation and Land Use Practices

**Erosion** is the wearing away of soil by water, wind, or ice, which is a natural process that has been accelerated by agricultural methods. Soil erosion takes place everywhere in the world, but some areas are more exposed and have a higher degree of erosion than others. Erosion occurs mostly in regions where vegetation has been removed. Deforestation and desertification leave land open to erosion.

In order to maintain the proper soil and nutrients for crop growth, land converted to agricultural use must experience only minimal soil erosion. Therefore, many techniques are used to protect soil from eroding and to minimize the loss of topsoil. Some soil quality management components include enhancement of organic matter, avoidance of excess tillage, efficient management of pests and soil nutrients, prevention of soil compaction, coverage of the ground so soil is not exposed, and diversification of cropping systems.

Several land use practices can also help to control soil erosion.

- **Contour farming**, or tilling at right angles to the slope of the land, is a simple method of preventing soil erosion and is useful on gentle slopes. Each ridge produced at right angles to the slope acts as a dam to prevent water from running down the slope. Therefore, more water soaks into the soil and less soil is washed away.
- **Strip farming** helps prevent erosion on longer or steeper slopes. Strips of closely sown crops are alternated with strips of row crops. The closely sown crops such as hay or wheat slow down the flow of water, reducing soil erosion.
- **Terracing** is a method of preventing soil erosion on steep land. Terraces are constructed at right angles to the slope.

- **Waterways** are depressions of land on sloped ground where water collects. Instead of allowing the land to remain bare, it should be properly maintained with a sod covering. Then, the speed of water flow is reduced and erosion is decreased.
- **Windbreaks** should be established to stop wind from eroding soil. Windbreaks are plantings of trees or other plants that protect soil from wind.

Methods of tilling the land, such as reduced tillage and conservation tillage, also help to reduce the amount of soil erosion. There are several variations of conservation tillage, including mulch tillage, strip tillage, ridge tillage, and no-till farming.

## Air Pollution Control

Because humans produce air pollution, it can be controlled by changes in human activity. Motor vehicles (including ships and airplanes) are the primary cause of air pollution, including $CO_2$ , carbon monoxide, volatile organic compounds, and nitrogen oxides ($NO_x$). Ozone is a secondary pollutant of motor vehicle use. Even though newer cars emit less nitrogen oxides, the mileage that people drive each year has increased, so $NO_x$ emissions have stayed the same. Almost all other air pollutants have been reduced significantly. Catalytic converters and an end to leaded gasoline also drastically improved air quality from automobile emissions. In an effort to reduce emissions in the United States, the mandatory fuel efficient standard for cars has slowly increased. Some manufacturers have introduced low or even zero emissions vehicles that rely partially or completely on electricity instead of fossil fuels.

Vehicle emissions can also be reduced through more compact development, improved mass transit, the increased cost of driving through tolls, or even direct bans on driving. Some Chinese cities only allow cars with even numbered license plates to drive some days and odd numbered plates to drive on other days as a way to lower the overall number of cars on the road.

Particulate matter emissions come from industrial activities, mining, farming, and the transfer of grain and coal. Improper land use is also a major source of airborne particulates, as is the burning of fossil fuels and wood. Technological fixes such as scrubbers are used by industries to trap particulate matter so it does not escape from smokestacks, but smaller particles that form sulfur dioxide and nitrogen oxides can still escape.

Power plant emissions of sulfur dioxide are also a cause of air pollution. Switching to the use of low-sulfur coal decreases emissions by about 66 percent. Switching to oil, natural gas, or nuclear fuels reduces emissions even more. It is also possible to reduce the sulfur in coal before it is used, but this process is costly and would drive up the cost of electricity. One benefit of these changes is a major reduction in acid rain.

Various policies aim to curb air pollution, such as regulations requiring natural gas refineries to reduce methane leakage.

## Drinking Water Quality and Supply

Drinking water supplies in the United States come mainly from municipal sources. About 37 percent of municipal water comes from wells, and the rest is surface water contained in reservoirs. In rural areas, residents obtain water from private wells.

To ensure water quality safety, water is treated by the following processes: raw water is filtered through sand or other substrates to remove particulate matter; chemicals are added to remove dissolved particles; and water is disinfected with chlorine, ozone, or UV light to remove organisms. When fresh water is scarce, saltwater can be treated through desalination processes and made suitable for drinking.

## Wastewater Treatment

Wastewater consists of storm water runoff, waste from industry, and domestic wastewater. Domestic waste consists primarily of organic matter from food preparation; garbage; washing clothes, dishes, and cars; and human waste. All wastewater must be cleaned before it is released, and, therefore, most municipalities and industries have wastewater treatment facilities.

Sewage treatment is classified as primary, secondary, and tertiary.

- **Primary** sewage treatment is a physical process that removes larger particles by filtering water through large screens and smaller particles by allowing them to settle out of the water as it sits in large tanks or lagoons. Water is removed from above the settled particles and is either released back into the environment or to another treatment stage.
- **Secondary** sewage treatment involves the holding of wastewater until all of the organic matter dissolved in the water is degraded by bacteria and other microorganisms. To promote the growth of microorganisms during this treatment stage, wastewater is mixed with highly oxygenated water, or it is aerated

directly with a trickling filter system. Microorganisms eventually settle out of the water in the form of sewage sludge. Water and sludge are separated, and the water is disinfected, usually with chlorine, before it is released.

- **Tertiary** treatment involves techniques to remove inorganic nutrients such as phosphorus and nitrogen in the water that could potentially increase aquatic plant growth.

## Solid and Hazardous Waste

Solid waste is garbage, sludge, refuse or any other discarded material resulting from industrial, agricultural, commercial mining, or municipal process. Solid waste can be solid, but it can also be liquid, semisolid, or even partially gaseous. Nations with high standards of living generally produce more solid waste than less developed nations.

There are several ways that humans dispose of solid waste. Landfills have been the primary means of solid waste disposal. Municipal solid waste landfills are constructed above impermeable clay layers lined with impermeable membranes. Each layer of garbage is covered with fresh soil to keep it from blowing away and to discourage scavengers. Contaminated water is trapped by leachate bottom layers. Decomposing waste does produce methane, which can be captured for use as an energy source.

Burning refuse in incinerators is another disposal method. Most incinerators are designed to capture thermal energy to make steam that is then used to produce electricity. Organic solid waste can be mulched or composted, and then reused in enriching soils or landscaping. Many municipalities now have composting facilities.

Hazardous wastes are by-products of certain industrial, business, or domestic activities that cannot be disposed of by normal measures. Waste is defined as hazardous if it causes or contributes to an increase in mortality or serious illness, or if it poses a serious threat to human health or the environment.

Hazardous waste ranges from waste containing dioxins and heavy metals to organic wastes. Hazardous waste can be liquid or in the form of batteries, computer parts, or CFL light bulbs.

Once a hazardous material has been identified, government agencies such as the Food and Drug Administration (FDA) and Occupational Safety and Health Administration (OSHA) determine acceptable exposure limits to the materials. Hazardous wastes can enter the environment, for example, by evaporating into the atmosphere or leaking through faulty pipes or improper disposal. Industries are now required to report the level of hazardous toxic waste released into the atmosphere.

Management of hazardous waste materials has become part of industrial processes, but the best way to deal with it is not to produce hazardous waste materials in the first place. The two most common methods of disposing of hazardous waste are incineration and land disposal, with land disposal being the primary disposal method.

Land disposal is carried out in four different ways:

1. Deep-well injection
2. Discharge of treated and untreated liquids into sewers or waterways
3. Placement of liquid or sludge in surface pits or lagoons
4. Storage of solid waste in specially designed landfills

## Recycling and Resource Recovery

Recycling efforts, including composting of organic materials, vary around the world. As of 2015, the United States recycled about 34 percent of its waste; Germany had one of the highest rates at 62 percent. In the United States, container laws set in 1972 have provided an economic incentive to recycle. These laws include a two- to five-cent deposit on all recyclable beverage containers. This law reduced beverage container litter by almost 50 percent. Mandatory recycling laws are in effect in many cities and states. Municipalities often provide recycling containers and curbside recycling to assist residents.

Although recycling programs have been successful at reducing waste, there are some economic and technical problems associated with recycling. For example, plastics are recyclable, but each type of plastic requires different recycling methods, and, therefore, all plastics cannot be recycled together. Also, recycling of materials has produced an overabundance of those materials, especially in developing nations.

To help reduce waste, people can buy materials that last, have goods repaired instead of discarding them, buy items that are reusable or recyclable, buy beverages in reusable glass containers, take reusable lunchboxes instead of paper bags, use rechargeable batteries, reduce the use of disposable bags, separate recyclables from trash, recycle all recyclable materials, choose items with minimal packaging, compost organic materials, and use electronic sources as opposed to paper sources. Most effective of all, people can try to consume less overall.

## Environmental Risk Assessment

Risk to the environment from human activities can be determined through identifying potential hazards and the consequences of these hazards. The magnitude and probability of the consequences also need to be considered when assessing risk. Finally, there needs to be an evaluation of the risk, also known as **risk characterization**. A concept frequently used in environmental risk assessment is that of source-pathway-receptor. The pathway between a hazard (source) and a receptor (i.e., ecosystem) is investigated. If no pathway exists, then there is no risk to the environment. If a pathway links a source to a receptor, then the consequences need to be assessed.

# SOCIAL PROCESSES AND THE ENVIRONMENT

Approximately 20 percent of the questions on the DSST Environmental Science exam will cover topics under the umbrella of social processes and the environment.

## Environmental Justice

Environmental justice is the idea that everyone is entitled to a clean environment regardless of race, income, class, or any other factor. Environmental responsibilities and benefits should be shared equally among all people.

All too often, the burden of environmental hazards falls most heavily on low-income communities, often racial or ethnic minorities. Polluting factories or waste sites are more likely to be located in low-income areas. In the United States, rates of asthma are much higher among communities of color, a trend partially attributable to greater exposure to outdoor and indoor air pollution. Much of the world's electronics recycling and disposal takes place in developing nations in West Africa, where low-wage workers extract valuable components without proper safety procedures or equipment. Across the world, low-income areas often lack political influence to successfully advocate for a clean and safe environment.

The Memphis Sanitation Strike of 1968 is seen as the first major environmental justice action in the United States. The 2014 Flint Water Crisis, where the city of Flint, Michigan, endured excessive lead in their drinking water supply, is a recent environmental justice concern.

Today, most federal and state environmental agencies are aware of the environmental justice problem and have initiated procedures, policies, and working groups such as the National Environmental Justice Advisory Council (NEJAC) to try and address the disparity. Despite the awareness, environmental justice continues to be a major problem in the United States, and other countries.

## Policy, Planning, and Decision Making

In the United States, the turn of the 20th century marked the beginning of federal policy to protect and conserve the environment. The Lacey Act, enacted in 1900, is considered the first environmental law in the United States, and was passed in response to widespread poaching and illegal wildlife harvesting. The act prohibits trade in illegally taken fish, wildlife, or plant products. A major turning point in the conservation of open space was the designation of protected state and national parks beginning in the late 19th century.

The publication of Rachel Carson's *Silent Spring* is considered the beginning of the modern environmental movement. In 1970, with the advent of Earth Day and mounting public concern for the environment, the United States began to address some of the most obvious and pressing environmental problems. Over the last 45 years, important environmental laws, like the Clean Air Acts, Clean Water Acts, Resource Conservation and Recovery Act, Energy Policy Act, land use conservation acts and more, have helped to protect the environment, wildlife species, and human populations. Many of these laws have been amended multiple times.

One notable act is the Comprehensive Environmental Response, Compensation, and Liability Act of 1980, also known as the Superfund. This act's main purpose is to clean up abandoned or unmonitored hazardous waste sites, and where possible, identify the party responsible for polluting the site and have them pay for the cleanup. Abandoned site cleanups are paid for out of a trust fund established by the act.

The Endangered Species Act (ESA), signed in 1973, provides legal protection to threatened species including their habitat and ecosystems. Species are covered by the act after a review.

Until 1970, most federal agencies acted within their authority without considering the environment, but the National Environmental Policy Act (NEPA) was designed to institutionalize within the federal government a concern for the environment. As a result of NEPA, many states have instituted stronger state environmental policy acts (SEPA). States may set and enforce their own environmental laws in addition to any federal laws. Congress established the Environmental Protection Agency (EPA) in 1970. The EPA helps to shape environmental laws and controls the daily operations of industries and regulates the agencies authorized to protect the environment, often in concert with state regulators. Water quality standards (for non–drinking water), for example, are set by states, subject to EPA approval. The EPA also has direct control over several aspects of the environment, including the research and regulation of pesticides. Drinking water standards are also set directly by the EPA under the Safe Drinking Water Act.

## Global Environmental Governance

Environmental concerns are a growing factor in international relations. Policies related to health, environmental, and natural resource concerns are beginning to enter the mainstream of political policies. There are many international institutions that address the global environment by gathering and evaluating environmental data, helping to develop international treaties, and providing funding and loans to developing countries.

Perhaps the most influential organization that has helped shape environmental policy is the United Nations (UN). The UN has 21 agencies that deal with environmental issues. Organizations formed under the UN include the UN Environment Programme (UNEP), the World Health Organization (WHO), the UN Development Programme (UNDP), and the Food and Agriculture Organization (FAO). However, some agencies fail to make significant progress because they are controlled by members with competing interests. Other institutions don't succeed because they are unable to address issues in their totality. For example, the World Bank can only address issues of air pollution and biodiversity for development projects that rely on funds from the World Bank.

Other organizations that influence environmental decisions are the Global Environment Facility (GEF) and the World Conservation Union (IUCN). All of these and other organizations have played a role in the following:

- Expanding the understanding of environmental issues
- Gathering and evaluating environmental data
- Developing international environmental treaties
- Providing funds for sustainable economic development in an attempt to reduce poverty
- Helping over 100 nations develop environmental laws and regulations

The International Organization for Standardization (ISO) was established in 1947 in Geneva to promote the development of voluntary standards for international trade. The ISO is a nongovernmental organization (NGO) that has developed over 10,000 standards that govern products. In the early 1990s, ISO began to work on standards for environmental management. These standards aim to do the following:

- Improve the understanding of the environmental impact of activities
- Have businesses comply with environmental regulations
- Prevent pollution
- Audit performance of businesses
- Set the standard of disclosing information about a business' environmental policy to the public

Despite tensions between domestic concerns, international relations, and environmental issues, there have been several successful international conventions and treaties that deal with the environment.

In 1987, the Montreal Protocol helped to start a decrease in CFCs in the atmosphere. The Earth Summit in 1992 aimed to develop better integration of national environmental goals with their economic goals. This summit led to the development of 27 principles to guide the behavior of nations toward better environmentally sustainable patterns; the adoption of Agenda 21; and a statement of principles for a global consensus on the management, conservation, and sustainable development of all types of forests. Later conferences have been less successful, with the major developing nations of China and India as well as the United States refusing to sign the Kyoto Protocol of 1997, while Canada withdrew in 2012. They Kyoto Protocol had some successes but did not succeed in lowering the global output of greenhouse emissions.

In 2016, 166 nations signed the Paris Agreement, where signing countries voluntarily agreed to each enact their own plan to reduce emissions to an increasingly low target. There was great flexibility in how a country might meet its emissions target, and there is no mechanism for enforcement or penalties if a target is not met. The United States withdrew from the agreement in 2017.

Like the Paris Agreement, most international environmental agreements are voluntary, in that countries must agree to participate. Most agreements are structured such that each individual participating nation has to set its own mechanisms and laws to meet the conditions of the agreement; the agreement does not replace national laws. Examples of international agreements structured this way are the 1995 Convention on Biological Diversity (CBD) or the Convention on International Trade in Endangered Species (CITES). In the case of CITES, several signatory nations do not have sufficient legal penalties to deter the illegal wildlife trade.

The world's oceans also provide areas of international cooperation. By the Law of the Sea, each coastal nation is allowed exclusive access to the waters up to 200 miles outwards from their coastline. The Law of the Sea treaty also provides guidelines for pollution prevention, marine research, and fisheries management, among others areas of international concern. Another example is the international ban on commercial whaling by the International Whaling Commission (IWC), enacted in 1986 and still in force despite several attempts to overturn it. There are also efforts to establish international marine protected areas (MPAs).

The European Union also works to maintain strict environmental standards for European countries. By 2000, more than 12 countries had adopted the policy of providing consumers with informational labels that enable them to be "green" consumers. Major corporations increasingly operate across national borders and have a major role to play in global conservation.

## Differing Cultural and Societal Values

Many people, either within the same culture or in different cultures, differ in their views about the environment. People with widely different worldviews can examine the same data and arrive at different conclusions because they view the problem with different assumptions and values. Some environmental worldviews are human-centered, whereas others are life-centered.

According to the human-centered worldview, humans are the most important species and should manage Earth to their benefit, no matter how it might affect other species. Another human-centered view is the stewardship worldview, in which it is believed that humans have the responsibility to care for and manage the Earth. According to this view, we are borrowing resources from the Earth and have the ethical responsibility to leave the Earth in at least as good a condition as we now enjoy.

Those with a life-centered worldview believe we have an ethical responsibility—not just for humans, but for all species—not to degrade Earth's ecosystems, biodiversity, and biosphere.

Which worldview a person possesses is to a large extent personal, but economic development can play a role. Many developing countries, aware that other developing countries already spent decades or centuries degrading their environment to reach their current level of development, often feel that they should have the ability to take the same path and develop to a high level before worrying as much about environmental concerns. It is also more difficult to worry about broader environmental damage when immediate survival is a concern. Poverty can drive a human-centered view and sometimes contributes to more harmful development practices.

The message of environmentalism for the future should be one of hope. It calls for a commitment to overcoming today's challenges regarding the environment with respect to world population, pollution, energy sources, and food supplies. The environmental revolution that many environmental scientists hope to achieve in this century has the following components:

- A biodiversity protection revolution
- An efficiency revolution
- A sufficiency revolution
- An energy revolution
- A pollution prevention revolution
- A demographic revolution
- An economic and political revolution

# SUMMING IT UP

- **Ecosystems** are a complex network of interrelationships between abiotic and biotic factors.
- A **community** consists of all interacting populations of various species living in a given area at the same time.
- There are three types of organisms in organism relationships: **predation**, **competition**, and **symbiosis**.
- There are three broad categories of organisms: **producers**, **consumers**, and **decomposers**.
- All organisms occupy one or more **trophic** levels, and available energy decreases as the trophic level increases.
- A **food chain** or **food web** describes the relationship of organisms within an ecosystem.
- **Biogeochemical cycling** is the process by which the most fit and best adapted members of a species survive and reproduce.
- **Succession** is a series of changes that ecosystems go through in order to maintain the stability of a community.
- **Biomes** are climax communities that are distributed around the world. In general, the structure of ecosystems within a given type of biome is similar.
- **Aquatic ecosystems** are shaped by the ability of the sun's energy to reach organisms below the water's surface, the depth to the bottom, the water's temperature, the amount of salts dissolved in the water, and the nature of the body of water.
- **Population biology** is concerned with the characterization of the make-up, growth, and impact of a population on the environment and its organisms.
- Earth's **atmosphere** is 78.1 percent nitrogen, 20.9 percent oxygen, and 1 percent other gases, including carbon dioxide, methane, and water vapor.
- There are four layers in Earth's atmosphere: **troposphere**, **stratosphere**, **mesosphere**, and **thermosphere**.
- **Human population growth** has a significant impact on the environment and a country's resources.
- **Developed** countries tend to have **low** rates of population growth, and **developing** countries tend to have **higher** rates of population growth.
- **Pollution** is a form of matter or energy that harms the environment.
- The **ozone layer** is necessary to block harmful UV light, but it is slowly being depleted by human activities.
- The **greenhouse effect** is necessary to keep Earth's temperature warm enough to sustain life. Since the Industrial Revolution, the concentration of **greenhouse gases** has increased in the atmosphere, increasing the amount

of heat being absorbed. The increase in the Earth's surface temperature will have a variety of impacts on climate and local weather. The effects will not be identical across the planet.

- **The Industrial Revolution** brought about the use of coal as a fuel source and the advent of machines, both of which caused a significant increase in pollution.

- **The Agricultural Revolution** developed techniques of growing larger quantities of food, especially after the invention of mechanized farm equipment.

- Agricultural practices can lead to **deforestation** and **desertification**, especially in developing countries. Agricultural and industrial runoff can lead to the process of **eutrophication** in aquatic environments. Improper waste disposal can also destroy habitat.

- **Nonrenewable energy sources** constitute 86.5 percent of the world's energy consumption, and only 13.5 percent of our energy comes from renewable sources.

- **The Green Revolution** introduced new, faster growing and hardier plant varieties and improved farming methods. High yields were achieved through the use of chemical fertilizers, pesticides, and herbicides.

- Agricultural practices are dependent on soil type, land conditions, and economic conditions. **Fertilizers** increase crop yield, but they cause problems to the environment. **Pesticides** increase crop yield, but they are harmful to the environment and to humans and other species. **Alternative agricultural methods** aim to preserve the environment by using fewer or no chemicals.

- **Erosion** is a natural process, but some land use practices can accelerate erosion. Other practices help to control erosion.

- Human activity produces **air pollution**, but humans can help to control air pollution by changing activities and practices.

- **Water treatment techniques** are used to provide safe, clean drinking water and to clean up wastewater before it is released back into the environment. Solid and hazardous waste is disposed of in landfills or incinerated.

- **Recycling** helps to reduce the amount of solid waste, but there are some technical and economic problems associated with recycling.

- **Environmental justice** is the equal access to a clean and healthy environment regardless of income, race, creed, or any other factor. Low income, minority, and other marginalized communities often suffer the worst consequences from inadequate environmental protection. Governments are starting to address these concerns.

- **Environmental policy** consists of laws, rules, and regulations developed by government organizations to solve environmental problems. Both states and the federal government are involved.

- **International environmental policies** are established by the United Nations and other world organizations.
- People view environmental issues as **human-centered, stewardship-centered,** or **life-centered** issues.

# Chapter 4

# Environmental Science Post-Test

## POST-TEST ANSWER SHEET

| | | |
|---|---|---|
| 1. Ⓐ Ⓑ Ⓒ Ⓓ | 17. Ⓐ Ⓑ Ⓒ Ⓓ | 33. Ⓐ Ⓑ Ⓒ Ⓓ |
| 2. Ⓐ Ⓑ Ⓒ Ⓓ | 18. Ⓐ Ⓑ Ⓒ Ⓓ | 34. Ⓐ Ⓑ Ⓒ Ⓓ |
| 3. Ⓐ Ⓑ Ⓒ Ⓓ | 19. Ⓐ Ⓑ Ⓒ Ⓓ | 35. Ⓐ Ⓑ Ⓒ Ⓓ |
| 4. Ⓐ Ⓑ Ⓒ Ⓓ | 20. Ⓐ Ⓑ Ⓒ Ⓓ | 36. Ⓐ Ⓑ Ⓒ Ⓓ |
| 5. Ⓐ Ⓑ Ⓒ Ⓓ | 21. Ⓐ Ⓑ Ⓒ Ⓓ | 37. Ⓐ Ⓑ Ⓒ Ⓓ |
| 6. Ⓐ Ⓑ Ⓒ Ⓓ | 22. Ⓐ Ⓑ Ⓒ Ⓓ | 38. Ⓐ Ⓑ Ⓒ Ⓓ |
| 7. Ⓐ Ⓑ Ⓒ Ⓓ | 23. Ⓐ Ⓑ Ⓒ Ⓓ | 39. Ⓐ Ⓑ Ⓒ Ⓓ |
| 8. Ⓐ Ⓑ Ⓒ Ⓓ | 24. Ⓐ Ⓑ Ⓒ Ⓓ | 40. Ⓐ Ⓑ Ⓒ Ⓓ |
| 9. Ⓐ Ⓑ Ⓒ Ⓓ | 25. Ⓐ Ⓑ Ⓒ Ⓓ | 41. Ⓐ Ⓑ Ⓒ Ⓓ |
| 10. Ⓐ Ⓑ Ⓒ Ⓓ | 26. Ⓐ Ⓑ Ⓒ Ⓓ | 42. Ⓐ Ⓑ Ⓒ Ⓓ |
| 11. Ⓐ Ⓑ Ⓒ Ⓓ | 27. Ⓐ Ⓑ Ⓒ Ⓓ | 43. Ⓐ Ⓑ Ⓒ Ⓓ |
| 12. Ⓐ Ⓑ Ⓒ Ⓓ | 28. Ⓐ Ⓑ Ⓒ Ⓓ | 44. Ⓐ Ⓑ Ⓒ Ⓓ |
| 13. Ⓐ Ⓑ Ⓒ Ⓓ | 29. Ⓐ Ⓑ Ⓒ Ⓓ | 45. Ⓐ Ⓑ Ⓒ Ⓓ |
| 14. Ⓐ Ⓑ Ⓒ Ⓓ | 30. Ⓐ Ⓑ Ⓒ Ⓓ | 46. Ⓐ Ⓑ Ⓒ Ⓓ |
| 15. Ⓐ Ⓑ Ⓒ Ⓓ | 31. Ⓐ Ⓑ Ⓒ Ⓓ | 47. Ⓐ Ⓑ Ⓒ Ⓓ |
| 16. Ⓐ Ⓑ Ⓒ Ⓓ | 32. Ⓐ Ⓑ Ⓒ Ⓓ | 48. Ⓐ Ⓑ Ⓒ Ⓓ |

49. Ⓐ Ⓑ Ⓒ Ⓓ        53. Ⓐ Ⓑ Ⓒ Ⓓ        57. Ⓐ Ⓑ Ⓒ Ⓓ

50. Ⓐ Ⓑ Ⓒ Ⓓ        54. Ⓐ Ⓑ Ⓒ Ⓓ        58. Ⓐ Ⓑ Ⓒ Ⓓ

51. Ⓐ Ⓑ Ⓒ Ⓓ        55. Ⓐ Ⓑ Ⓒ Ⓓ        59. Ⓐ Ⓑ Ⓒ Ⓓ

52. Ⓐ Ⓑ Ⓒ Ⓓ        56. Ⓐ Ⓑ Ⓒ Ⓓ        60. Ⓐ Ⓑ Ⓒ Ⓓ

# ENVIRONMENTAL SCIENCE POST-TEST

**Directions:** Carefully read each of the following 60 questions. Choose the best answer to each question and fill in the corresponding circle on the answer sheet. The Answer Key and Explanations can be found following this post-test.

1. Which of the following is a predicted impact of global climate change?

   A. Greater sea ice cover at the North Pole
   B. Increased acid deposition
   C. More intense storms
   D. Ozone depletion

2. Which of the following is an essential practice in maintaining good soil quality for farming?

   A. Keeping the ground covered
   B. Keeping crops consistent
   C. Tilling the land frequently
   D. Compacting the soil

3. What would the population profile look like in a country in the first stage of the demographic transition?

   A. Many children, intermediate number of working-age adults, fewer elderly
   B. Many adults, fewer children, fewer elderly
   C. Few children, few working-age adults, many elderly
   D. Many adults, many children, more elderly

4. One consequence of introducing agricultural technology to a developing country is

   A. an increased carrying capacity.
   B. a decreased carrying capacity.
   C. a steady carrying capacity.
   D. no effect on carrying capacity.

**5.** Degradation of ecosystems and loss of biodiversity in emerging nations is most often due to

**A.** overgrowth of vegetation.
**B.** development.
**C.** flooding.
**D.** poor soil quality.

**6.** Which of the following gases is thought to be a major contributor to the effect of global climate change?

**A.** $NO_2$
**B.** $SO_2$
**C.** $CO_2$
**D.** $O_3$

**7.** Where is secondary succession likely to occur?

**A.** On a bare rock surface
**B.** Land covered by floods
**C.** Islands created by volcanoes
**D.** A sandy beach

**8.** Mycorrhizal fungi live among plant roots, increasing nutrient and water access for the plants in exchange for carbohydrates. Such a relationship is best described as

**A.** mutualism.
**B.** commensalism.
**C.** parasitism.
**D.** competition.

**9.** Which of the following is an example of a life-centered worldview?

**A.** Maintaining protected areas for wildlife
**B.** Providing financial subsidies for industry
**C.** Teaching sustainable development in schools
**D.** Providing forested land free to farmers

**10.** Which of the following is generally true about soil erosion?

   **A.** The amount of topsoil remains relatively constant over long periods of time.
   **B.** Soil is eroding faster than it forms.
   **C.** There are no effective methods to prevent soil erosion.
   **D.** As soil erodes, new soil replaces it.

**11.** Which of the following is the correct order in a simple four-step food chain?

   **A.** Producer, tertiary consumer, secondary consumer, primary consumer
   **B.** Primary consumer, secondary consumer, tertiary consumer, producer
   **C.** Producer, primary consumer, secondary consumer, tertiary consumer
   **D.** Tertiary consumer, secondary consumer, primary consumer, producer

**12.** Which of the following is an example of a point source of water pollution?

   **A.** Urban street runoff
   **B.** A discharge pipe
   **C.** Acid rain
   **D.** Eroding stream banks

**13.** Which of the following is NOT an environmental justice issue?

   **A.** A new landfill placed in a lower-income community
   **B.** Exporting hazardous waste to a developing nation
   **C.** A new corporate headquarters located in an urban area
   **D.** Poor water quality in a predominantly minority area

**14.** The living components of an ecosystem are called

   **A.** biotic factors.
   **B.** abiotic factors.
   **C.** environmental factors.
   **D.** biosphere factors.

15. The ozone layer is a necessary part of the atmosphere protecting Earth's surface from

   A. meteors.
   B. air pollution.
   C. carbon monoxide.
   D. ultraviolet light.

16. What percent of the world's electrical power comes from nonrenewable energy sources and nuclear energy?

   A. 91 percent
   B. 87 percent
   C. 9 percent
   D. 4 percent

17. What is one potential consequence of unequal access to a clean environment?

   A. Nuclear accidents
   B. Declining availability of landfill space
   C. Dirty fuel power plants
   D. Higher rates of respiratory disease

18. Which phenomenon is necessary to keep Earth warm enough to sustain life?

   A. Biodiversity
   B. Global warming
   C. The greenhouse effect
   D. Depleting ozone layer

19. A primary goal of the Superfund is to

   A. clean up hazardous waste sites.
   B. apply certain requirements to storm water discharge.
   C. prohibit ocean dumping.
   D. gain control of point source pollution.

20. In a temperate deciduous forest, maple trees, birds, and squirrels all live in the same given area. All three species together make up a(n)

   A. ecosystem.
   B. community.
   C. population.
   D. niche.

21. The total fertility rate of a population is the

   A. number of births and deaths.
   B. fertility rate necessary to replace a generation.
   C. number of children born to each woman in her lifetime.
   D. number of women of childbearing age.

22. Which of the following is an example of a persistent pesticide?

   A. DDT
   B. Diazinon
   C. Organophosphates
   D. Carbamates

23. What is one way that differing social views might make environmental protection decisions more difficult?

   A. People with opposing viewpoints cooperate easily.
   B. People with opposing viewpoints come to identical conclusions from the same information.
   C. People with opposing viewpoints always find common ground.
   D. People with opposing viewpoints can reach opposite conclusions using the same information.

24. Which of the following is NOT a feature of evolution?

   A. Limiting factors
   B. Extinction
   C. Genetic variation
   D. Natural selection

25. Which biome harbors the fewest species of plants?

   A. Tropical rainforest
   B. Tundra
   C. Wetlands
   D. Desert

26. In 1992, the Earth Summit aimed to develop a better integration of each country's environmental and

    A. ecological goals.
    B. biodiversity goals.
    C. economic goals.
    D. agricultural goals.

27. Which federal agency regulates the use of pesticides?

    A. Department of Agriculture
    B. Environmental Protection Agency
    C. National Institutes of Health
    D. Food and Drug Administration

28. Which of the following is an example of interspecific competition?

    A. Moss-tree
    B. Shark-remora
    C. Tapeworm-dog
    D. Hawk-owl

29. Which of the following are among the first organisms that may appear in secondary succession?

    A. Grasses
    B. Autotrophs
    C. Lichen
    D. Shrubs

30. Mass production contributed most to which major environmental concern?

    A. Habitat destruction
    B. Global climate change
    C. Solid waste
    D. Water pollution

31. Which fuel source can be produced from biomass materials that contain cellulose or starch?

    A. Carbon dioxide
    B. Coal
    C. Ethanol
    D. Oil

32. Improvements to the combustion engine have decreased which type of air pollution?

    A. Sulfur dioxide
    B. Volatile organic compounds
    C. Oxides of nitrogen
    D. Carbon monoxide

33. Which of the following is a possible difficulty of recycling plastics?

    A. It requires fossil fuels.
    B. It causes an increase in pollution.
    C. All types of plastic cannot be recycled by the same methods.
    D. Most municipalities do not recycleplastic.

34. Which of the following is NOT a source of acid deposition?

    A. Automobiles
    B. Trees
    C. Farm animals
    D. Factories

35. Which of the following statements most accurately describes the role of nitrifying-fixing bacteria in the nitrogen cycle?

    A. It converts ammonia to nitrites and nitrates.
    B. It converts nitrites to nitrogen gas.
    C. It incorporates nitrates into amino acid.
    D. It converts nitrogen gas into ammonia.

36. Which of the following is indicative of a high genetic diversity in a given population?

    A. Varied structures and abilities
    B. Uniform structures and abilities
    C. Highly evolved individuals
    D. Varied ecosystems

37. Which would be the best way to help permanently ensure environmental justice for a low-income community?

    A. Increase political representation
    B. Change zoning laws
    C. Provide free bottled water
    D. Retrofit old buildings

**38.** Organisms that obtain nutrition at all trophic levels are

    **A.** producers.
    **B.** carnivores.
    **C.** decomposers.
    **D.** herbivores.

**39.** The exploitation of minerals in oceans is controlled by the

    **A.** United Nations.
    **B.** Clean Water Act.
    **C.** Resource Conservation and Recovery Act.
    **D.** Law of the Sea.

**40.** Which of the following processes provides usable energy to producers?

    **A.** Photosynthesis
    **B.** Cellular respiration
    **C.** Digestion
    **D.** Osmosis

**41.** Which process of irrigation conserves the most water?

    **A.** Gravity-flow irrigation
    **B.** Flood irrigation
    **C.** Trickle irrigation
    **D.** Center-pivot irrigation

**42.** Which listed feature is the defining characteristic of a desert biome?

    **A.** High temperature
    **B.** Low biodiversity
    **C.** Sand dunes
    **D.** Low rainfall

**43.** Surface mining regulations require that land damaged from the effects of surface mining must be

    **A.** filled with topsoil when the mine is shut down.
    **B.** replanted with vegetation.
    **C.** converted to an artificial lake.
    **D.** cleaned and decontaminated.

44. What is the primary mechanism for setting standards for non-drinking water?

    A. The EPA sets all water quality standards.
    B. Standards are set only at the state level.
    C. The EPA approves each state's standards.
    D. Standards are set directly by an act of Congress.

45. Which of the following is an international organization that plays a major role in environmental conservation?

    A. CITES
    B. IUCN
    C. EPA
    D. UNICEF

46. Which act sets environmental policies at the state level?

    A. NEPA
    B. SEPA
    C. CERCLA
    D. CBD

47. Which of the following is a feature of sustainable agriculture?

    A. Planting multiple crops in the same field
    B. Use of fertilizers to increase crop growth
    C. Only planting in a field every other year
    D. Practicing monoculture

48. An endangered marine fish in coastal waters is protected by which law(s)?

    A. State law
    B. Marine Mammal Protection Act
    C. ESA
    D. Law of the Sea

49. Which of the following concepts is frequently used in environmental risk assessment?

    A. Pollution control
    B. Damage control
    C. Source-pathway-receptor
    D. Source-pathway-control

**50.** Two types of beetles live on the trunks of dead trees. Which best explains why brown beetles survive over green beetles in that situation?

**A.** Green beetles taste better to birds.
**B.** Brown beetles are less visible, so birds do not see them.
**C.** Brown beetles reproduce faster than green beetles.
**D.** It happens by chance.

**51.** The stewardship worldview of environmentalism maintains that

**A.** we must consider our neighbors' well-being.
**B.** we must care for all living creatures no matter how small.
**C.** we have a responsibility to care for Earth so it is preserved for future generations.
**D.** we are completely dependent on nature for our survival.

**52.** The first significant increase in atmospheric $CO_2$ levels is linked to

**A.** the thinning ozone layer above Antarctica.
**B.** the warming of ocean temperatures.
**C.** an increase in vegetation on Earth.
**D.** the Industrial Revolution.

**53.** Which scientific practice yields plants with desired traits?

**A.** Mutation
**B.** Selective crossbreeding
**C.** Chemical enhancement
**D.** Sustainable farming

**54.** Human populations can best be described as

**A.** r-strategists.
**B.** l-strategists.
**C.** k-strategists.
**D.** survivalists.

55. Which of the following describes the method of contour farming?

   A. Tilling only in a narrow region that is to receive seeds while all other soil is undisturbed
   B. Farming at right angles to a slope of land
   C. Diversifying crops planted in given area
   D. Leaving a ridge the previous year and planting the new crop in the ridge

56. What is one environmental problem that arose from the Agricultural Revolution?

   A. Soil erosion
   B. Air pollution
   C. Poor crop yield
   D. Increase in pests

57. Which of the following describes limiting factors?

   A. A factor that determines the fertility rate of an organism
   B. Always an intrinsic factor
   C. An environmental factor that determines size of a population
   D. Independent of the environment

58. The largest proportion of deforestation is caused by

   A. acid rain.
   B. drought.
   C. agricultural development.
   D. forest fires.

59. Which energy source can be obtained from a landfill?

   A. Ethane
   B. Hydrogen
   C. Methane
   D. Steam

60. In which area of the world listed below is desertification most prevalent?

   A. Western United States
   B. Northern Africa
   C. Eastern Europe
   D. Central America

# ANSWER KEY AND EXPLANATIONS

| | | | | |
|---|---|---|---|---|
| 1. C | 13. C | 25. B | 37. A | 49. C |
| 2. A | 14. A | 26. C | 38. C | 50. B |
| 3. A | 15. D | 27. B | 39. D | 51. C |
| 4. A | 16. A | 28. D | 40. A | 52. D |
| 5. B | 17. D | 29. A | 41. C | 53. B |
| 6. C | 18. C | 30. C | 42. D | 54. C |
| 7. B | 19. A | 31. C | 43. B | 55. B |
| 8. A | 20. B | 32. D | 44. C | 56. A |
| 9. A | 21. C | 33. C | 45. B | 57. C |
| 10. B | 22. A | 34. C | 46. B | 58. C |
| 11. C | 23. D | 35. A | 47. A | 59. C |
| 12. B | 24. A | 36. A | 48. C | 60. B |

1. **The correct answer is C.** Storms are predicted to increase in strength as a result of global climate change since there will be warmer ocean waters providing more energy to feed them. Note that it is difficult to link the strength of any given storm to climate change. Choice A is incorrect since ice cover is decreasing at the poles, not increasing. Choices B and D are incorrect since both acid deposition and ozone depletion are concerns that are mostly unrelated to greenhouse gases or climate change.

2. **The correct answer is A.** Bare soil is susceptible to wind and water erosion, so groundcover protects soil, provides habitats for larger soil organisms like earthworms, and can improve water availability to surrounding areas. Choice B is incorrect because the practice of crop rotation, rather than planting the same crop each year, is more beneficial to the soil. Choice C is incorrect because frequent tilling is actually damaging to soil and should be avoided. Choice D is incorrect because compaction reduces the amount of air, water, and space available to plant roots and soil organisms, so it should be avoided in order to maintain soil quality.

3. **The correct answer is A.** The first stage of the demographic transition is marked by high birthrates and high death rates. Such populations will have many young children but fewer elderly people. Choice B is characteristic of a country much later in the transition when birthrates have started to drop but the population has not yet begun to age. Choice C is a population in which birthrates have fallen below replacement level and adults are aging faster than more children are born. Choice D is a population in stage 2 of the transition, when birthrates are still high but death rates have fallen.

4. **The correct answer is A.** The carrying capacity within an environment can increase through advances in agricultural technology. Choice B is incorrect because the introduction of agricultural technology would increase, not decrease, the carrying capacity. Choice C is incorrect because there would be a continual increase in carrying capacity, not a leveling off. Choice D is incorrect because agricultural technology would affect the carrying capacity in a positive way.

5. **The correct answer is B.** Development, whether for industry or urban growth, in emerging nations can lead to loss of biodiversity and ecosystem degradation. Choice A is incorrect because an overgrowth of vegetation, even if it replaces native habitat, is still a typically better habitat than land that is built upon. Choice C is incorrect because flooding is not the major cause of loss of biodiversity or ecosystem degradation in emerging nations. Choice D is incorrect because poor soil quality is a possible consequence of industrial development.

6. **The correct answer is C.** Carbon dioxide ($CO_2$) is the most abundant of greenhouse gases, and it is thought to be a major contributor to global climate change. Choice A is incorrect because nitrous oxide, not nitrogen dioxide, is a greenhouse gas. Choice B is incorrect because sulfur dioxide is produced when fossil fuels are burned, and it is not a greenhouse gas. Choice D is incorrect because ozone is not a greenhouse gas, so it doesn't contribute to global climate change.

7. **The correct answer is B.** Secondary succession begins with the disturbance of an existing ecosystem. Floodwaters can cause heavy damage to ecosystems, providing an opening for new types of plant growth. Choices A, C, and D are not the best answers because these are all areas where there is likely a lack of organisms and primary succession would occur first.

8. **The correct answer is A.** The relationship is mutualistic when both species benefit from the relationship. Fungi and plant roots both benefit from the association. The fungus obtains organic materials from the plant roots, and the branched nature of the fungus assists the plant in obtaining nutrients from the soil. Choice B is incorrect because in this relationship only one organism benefits, while the other is unaffected. Choice C is incorrect because in this relationship, one organism obtains nourishment from a host organism, but in the process it may harm the host. Choice D is incorrect because the relationship doesn't represent a competition between the two species.

9. **The correct answer is A.** The life-centered view believes that there is an obligation to protect the biosphere and all the life in it; protected areas such as wildlife preserves would aid in that goal. Choices B and D are examples of a human-centered view. Choice C is an action that would be part of a stewardship view.

10. **The correct answer is B.** Every year, erosion carries away more topsoil than is formed; this occurs mostly because of agricultural practices that often leave soil unprotected from wind and water. Choice A is incorrect because some regions of the world lose significant amounts of soil over time. Choice C is incorrect because environmental scientists and conservationists work to reduce soil loss through many different soil conservation methods that have been effective in slowing the rate of erosion. Choice D is incorrect because soil erodes faster than it is replaced in nature.

11. **The correct answer is C.** The correct order of steps in a typical food chain is producer, primary consumer herbivore, secondary consumer omnivore or carnivore, tertiary consumer carnivore, and decomposer. Choices A, B, and D are incorrect because none of them represent the correct order of a typical food chain.

12. **The correct answer is B.** A discharge pipe is a point source of water pollution because the source of pollution is readily identified. Choices A, C, and D are incorrect because these are all examples of nonpoint sources of water pollution.

13. **The correct answer is C.** A corporate headquarters may be a boon to a local economy with minimal environmental impact. Such projects are usually sought out by municipal authorities and such development is not an environmental justice issue. Choices A, B, and D all involve conditions that might be hazardous to the environment or human health where the consequences are borne by a low-income or marginalized population.

14. **The correct answer is A.** Biotic factors are living organisms that interact with the environment. Choice B is incorrect because abiotic factors are nonliving components of an ecosystem; they are the matter, energy, and surrounding space that help to shape an environment. Choice C is incorrect because an environment encompasses all living and nonliving things interacting together. Choice D is incorrect because a biosphere is defined as the life zone of the Earth and includes all living organisms.

15. **The correct answer is D.** The ozone layer shields Earth from the harmful effects of ultraviolet light radiation. An intact ozone layer absorbs approximately 99 percent of ultraviolet (UV) light and prevents it from reaching Earth's surface. Choice A is incorrect because the ozone layer doesn't block meteor showers from reaching Earth. Choice B is incorrect because air pollution is found below the ozone layer of the atmosphere. Choice C is incorrect because carbon monoxide is a pollutant released into the atmosphere by activities on Earth's surface.

16. **The correct answer is A.** Nonrenewable fossil fuels and nuclear power provide 91 percent of the world's energy (87 percent fossil fuels, 4 percent nuclear). Choice B is incorrect because 87 percent of energy comes from nonrenewable energy sources alone. Choice C is incorrect because about 9 percent of the world's energy comes from renewable sources at this time, most of it hydroelectric. Choice D is incorrect because 4 percent of energy comes from nuclear energy alone.

17. **The correct answer is D.** Unequal access to a clean environment means some communities, usually low-income or minority communities, can experience more harm, such as respiratory disease from exposure to air pollution. Nuclear accidents (choice A) are an environmental justice issue if the accident only impacts certain populations. Choices B and C are not automatically problems that impact some communities more than others, but certainly they can be.

18. **The correct answer is C.** The greenhouse effect is necessary to sustain all life on Earth. Choice A is incorrect because although biodiversity *helps* to sustain a variety of life on Earth, it is not *necessary* to sustain all life. Choice B is incorrect because global warming can be harmful to life on Earth. Choice D is incorrect because the depleting ozone layer leads to global warming, not sustained life on Earth.

19. **The correct answer is A.** A primary goal of the Superfund Act is to clean up hazardous waste sites. Choice B is incorrect because it refers to a goal of the Water Quality Act. Choice C is incorrect because the prohibition against ocean dumping is a provision of the Marine Protection, Research, and Sanctuaries Act of 1988. Choice D is incorrect because it was the Clean Water Act of 1977 that first sought to gain control of point source pollution.

20. **The correct answer is B.** All the different populations living in a certain place make up a community. Choice A is incorrect because an ecosystem includes all living and nonliving things in an environment. Choice C is incorrect because each of the three species is a separate population. Different species cannot be part of the same population. Choice D is incorrect because the role of each organism in a community is its niche.

21. **The correct answer is C.** The total fertility rate of a population is the number of children born to each woman in her lifetime. Choice A is incorrect because the number of births and deaths in a population is not the total fertility rate. Choice B is not correct because this describes the replacement fertility rate. Choice D is incorrect because the number of women of childbearing age doesn't reflect the total fertility rate.

22. **The correct answer is A.** DDT is a chlorinated hydrocarbon, which is a type of persistent pesticide. Choice B is incorrect because diazinon is a widely used nonpersistent pesticide. Choice C is incorrect because organophosphates are nonpersistent insecticides in that they decompose quickly into harmless by-products. Organophospates aren't species-specific and will kill all insects, whether they are harmful or beneficial. Choice D is incorrect because carbamates are nonpersistent pesticides that work by interfering with an insect's nervous system.

23. **The correct answer is D.** When people approach environmental problems from very different viewpoints, they can all view the same information but draw different conclusions about the right action to take. Since solving environmental problems usually requires consensus, different social or cultural values can make solving problems more difficult. Choice A is incorrect since generally different viewpoints make cooperation more difficult. Choice B is incorrect since frequently opposing perspectives reach opposing conclusions. Choice C is incorrect since while common ground often exists between opposing viewpoints, there is no guarantee that it will be found.

24. **The correct answer is A.** Limiting factors are not a component of evolution. In general, this term refers to factors in an ecosystem that limit its success. Choice B is incorrect because extinction is a common feature of evolution. Choice C is incorrect because genetic variability is necessary for evolution to occur. Choice D is incorrect because natural selection is an important part of evolution. Natural selection is the process in which the individuals of a species best able to survive and reproduce will pass on traits that will continue to be expressed in a species. This process leads to evolution of species.

25. **The correct answer is B.** Not very many species of plants can survive in the conditions of the tundra; there are no large plants, so an entire category of plants and the diversity it adds is missing from that biome. Choice A is incorrect because a tropical rainforest provides a warm, wet climate that is advantageous to producing multiple species of plants of all types resulting in an extremely high diversity. Choice C is incorrect because wetlands are a diverse environment with varying soil types that are conducive to plant diversity. Choice D is incorrect because despite their reputation, most deserts are far from barren and hold a great diversity of plant and animal life.

26. **The correct answer is C.** The Earth Summit aimed to integrate environmental and economic goals of countries so choices A, B, and D are incorrect.

27. **The correct answer is B.** The EPA researches and regulates pesticide use, although individual states also have a role in pesticide licensing and regulation. Choices A, C, and D are incorrect because researching and regulating pesticides is not the function of any of these agencies.

28. **The correct answer is D.** Hawks and owls are both predators that compete for the same prey, including mice and rabbits. Because hawks and owls are different species, this is called interspecific competition. Choice A is incorrect because moss and trees have a commensal relationship; some moss benefits by growing on the base of a tree, but the tree is not affected. Choice B is incorrect because the shark and the remora have a commensal relationship in which the remora benefits and the shark is unaffected. Choice C is incorrect because the tapeworm is a parasite to the dog, not a predator.

29. **The correct answer is A.** Since the damaged area still has intact soil, it would undergo secondary succession, and grass would be one of the first organisms to grow. Choice B is incorrect because autotrophic microorganisms would appear in an area where there are no life forms and no intact soil. Choice C is incorrect because lichen would be one of the first organisms to appear during primary succession. Choice D is incorrect because in secondary succession, shrubs would appear after grasses.

30. **The correct answer is C.** Mass production enabled the replacement of durable goods with inexpensive disposable products, such as plastic bags, and facilitated greater consumption. Many of these products end up in landfills or as litter. Choices A, B, and D are incorrect since while all of these increased as a result of the industrial revolution, all industries played a role, not just mass production.

31. **The correct answer is C.** Ethanol is an alcohol used as a fuel source; it is produced by the fermentation of sugar, starch, or cellulose. Choice A is incorrect because carbon dioxide is not a fuel source. Choice B is incorrect because coal is produced over time and under high pressure from decaying organic matter. Choice D is incorrect because oil is a fuel source produced by oils released from the remains of marine organisms. Like coal, oil forms over a very long period of time.

32. **The correct answer is D.** Increased fuel efficiency and the use of catalytic converters have reduced carbon monoxide emissions. However, carbon monoxide pollution is still a problem because cars now drive greater distances and there are more cars on the road. Choices A, B, and C are incorrect because the level of all of these air pollutants is not affected by improvements in the combustion engine and catalytic converter.

33. **The correct answer is C.** Goods are manufactured using different types of plastic. All of these plastics need to be separated and recycled by different methods, which raises the price of recycling and might encourage disposal and waste instead of recycling. Choice A is incorrect because recycling doesn't require the use of fossil fuels. Choice B is incorrect because recycling can reduce air and water pollution. Choice D is incorrect because many municipalities have recycling programs.

34. **The correct answer is C.** Farm animals don't release any sulfur dioxide or oxides of nitrogen into the atmosphere. Choices A, B, and D are incorrect because they are all sources of acid deposition.

35. **The correct answer is A.** Nitrifying bacteria are able to convert ammonia in soil into nitrites and nitrates. Nitrogen-fixing bacteria are able to convert atmospheric nitrogen gas that enters the soil into ammonia that plants can use. Choice B is incorrect because denitrifying bacteria convert nitrites into nitrogen gas. Choice C is incorrect because the nitrates are taken up by plants and incorporated into amino acids. Choice D is incorrect because nitrogen-fixing bacteria are able to convert atmospheric nitrogen gas that enters the soil into ammonia that plants can use.

36. **The correct answer is A.** High genetic diversity is a level of biodiversity in which there is a great variation in genetic material within a population; therefore, individuals will have varied structure and abilities. Choice B is incorrect because low genetic diversity yields a population that was more uniform in structure and ability. Choice C is incorrect because high genetic diversity indicates variety of genes, but doesn't imply anything about the complexity of the organisms. Choice D is incorrect because a high genetic diversity doesn't imply varied ecosystems.

**37. The correct answer is A.** Reduced political influence is a major cause of environmental justice problems. Improving political representation to ensure that all communities have equal participation in the political process is one way to prevent future environmental problems. Changing zoning laws (choice B) might help, but only if the new laws make impactful development more difficult in affected neighborhoods. Unfortunately, zoning laws often perpetuate environmental injustice by limiting industrial development in marginalized areas. Choices C and D might help with immediate problems of dirty water or inefficient heat, but they are temporary solutions that will not permanently solve the problem of unequal access to a clean environment.

**38. The correct answer is C.** Decomposers are organisms that will feed off all other organisms within an ecosystem whenever those organisms shed, excrete waste, or die. Therefore, decomposers are capable of feeding off organisms at every trophic level. Choice A is incorrect because producers are plants and at the first trophic level. Choice B is incorrect because carnivores feed and occupy higher trophic levels only. Choice D is incorrect because herbivores occupy the second trophic level.

**39. The correct answer is D.** The Law of the Sea aims to create a legal mechanism for controlling the exploitation of mineral resources in open waters. Choice A is incorrect because the United Nations doesn't control the exploitation of minerals. The Clean Water Act (Choice B) regulates water pollution. Choice C is incorrect because the Resource Conservation and Recovery Act controls hazardous waste disposal.

**40. The correct answer is A.** During photosynthesis, carbon dioxide present in the atmosphere is taken in by plants and converted into glucose in a reaction powered by sunlight. Plants and animals—consumers—use the glucose as a source of energy. Choice B is incorrect because animals use the process of oxygen respiration to breathe and convert oxygen into carbon dioxide. Choice C is not correct because the process of digestion doesn't occur in plants. Choice D is incorrect because osmosis doesn't play a role in providing an energy source.

41. **The correct answer is C.** Trickle, or drip, irrigation is a very efficient method in which 90 to 95 percent of the water reaches the
crops. In this method, small flexible tubing is inserted at or below
ground level, and small holes in the tubing deliver water to the
plant roots. Choice A is incorrect because gravity-flow irrigation
consists of unlined ditches filled with water; the water flows by
gravity to the crops. Choice B is incorrect because flood irrigation
includes large ditches filled with water similar to gravity-flow irrigation. Choice D is incorrect because center-pivot irrigation systems use center-pivot sprinklers that move in a circular motion to
deliver water to crops, which uses a large amount of water.

42. **The correct answer is D.** Deserts are defined by the low amount
of precipitation they receive. Although deserts are thought of as
hot (choice A) it is not always the case and temperature does not
define a desert. Biodiversity (choice B) varies from desert to desert, but is usually quite high. Sand dunes (choice C) are not found
in all deserts.

43. **The correct answer is B.** The Surface Mining Control and Rec-
lamation Act of 1977 required that all mining companies replant
vegetation on land that was strip mined. Choice A is incorrect
because the land doesn't only need to be covered with topsoil,
but it must also have vegetation planted. Choice C is incorrect
because there is no regulation specifying that strip-mined land
be converted into lakes. Choice D is incorrect because the land
doesn't need to be decontaminated.

44. **The correct answer is C.** Each state may set its own standards for
non–drinking water, but the EPA must approve those standards.
Choice A is incorrect since the EPA only directly sets standards
for drinking water. Choice B is incorrect since each state is still
subject to federal oversight. Choice D is incorrect since Congress
empowered the EPA and the states to set and enforce water quality standards.

45. **The correct answer is B.** The International Union for the Conservation of Nature, or IUCN, is an international agency with the primary role of assessing the status of species and ecosystems and sharing advice about how to conserve them. CITES (choice A) is an international agreement but is not an organization. The EPA (choice C) is a US government agency, not an international one. UNICEF (choice D) is an international agency, but its primary mandate is childrens' rights and well-being, not environmental issues.

46. **The correct answer is B.** SEPA stands for State Environmental Policy Acts. These vary from state to state but are often stronger than federal regulations. Choices A and C are both national. CBD (choice D) is an international agreement.

47. **The correct answer is A.** In practices of sustainable agriculture, multiple crops are planted on the same plot and harvested at different times. Choice B is incorrect because sustainable agriculture doesn't promote the use of fertilizers or chemical pesticides. Choice C is incorrect because fields aren't left bare or unplanted. Choice D is incorrect because multiple crops are planted in one field.

48. **The correct answer is C.** Endangered species are protected by the ESA regardless of whether they inhabit state or federal territory, and ESA covers marine as well as terrestrial species. State law (choice A) is incorrect, for even though the fish inhabits state waters, it is protected primarily by ESA if it is endangered. The Marine Mammal Protection Act (choice B) does not apply to fish and is also not the primary law protecting endangered species. The Law of the Sea (choice D) does not apply to coastal waters other than to designate each country's Exclusive Economic Zone.

49. **The correct answer is C.** A concept frequently used in environmental risk assessment is that of source-pathway-receptor. The pathway between a hazard source and a receptor is investigated. If no pathway exists, then there is no risk to the environment. If a pathway links a source to a receptor, then the consequences need to be assessed. Choice A is incorrect because pollution control is an action taken to reduce a risk, not assess one. Choice B is incorrect because damage control isn't a way to assess environmental risks. Choice D is incorrect because control of a hazard isn't a means of assessment, but a means of reducing risk.

50. **The correct answer is B.** Dead tree trunks are brown; a brown beetle will be better camouflaged against the trunks, and less visible to predators such as birds. Therefore, the brown beetle is less likely to be eaten and more likely to live long enough to reproduce. This process of natural selection favors the brown beetle over the green beetle. Choice A is incorrect because the taste of the beetles is no different. Choice C is incorrect because the reproduction rate is no different. Choice D is incorrect because natural selection doesn't happen by chance.

51. **The correct answer is C.** The stewardship worldview maintains that people have an ethical responsibility to be good stewards of Earth and need to manage it well for future generations. Choice A is incorrect because this human-centered worldview focuses on future generations. Choice B is incorrect because the stewardship worldview is a human-centered view of the environment. Choice D is incorrect because this isn't part of the stewardship worldview.

52. **The correct answer is D.** A rapid increase of $CO_2$ in the atmosphere was first observed during the Industrial Revolution when there was a significant increase in the amount of coal burned for energy. Choice A is incorrect because the thinning of the ozone layer over Antarctica may be the result of an increase in $CO_2$, but it is not the cause of an increase in $CO_2$. Choice B is incorrect because warmer ocean temperatures don't increase $CO_2$. Choice C is incorrect because there is less vegetation in many areas, not more.

53. **The correct answer is B.** Selective crossbreeding is a method in which scientists cross-pollinate plants with desired traits until they generate seeds that will grow plants with the target desired traits. Choice A is incorrect because mutations wouldn't always produce desired traits. Choice C is incorrect because chemical enhancement isn't always a safe way to obtain plants with desired traits. Choice D is incorrect because sustainable farming is an agricultural practice of farming that doesn't use chemicals.

54. **The correct answer is C.** Humans can best be described as k-strategists because k-selected species have few offspring and spend a great deal of energy and time ensuring that their offspring survive to reproductive age. Choice A is incorrect because r-selected species have a large number of offspring and don't care for them after they are born. Choice B is incorrect because l-strategist is not a term relevant to population biology. Choice D is incorrect because survivalist is not a term used to describe human populations.

55. **The correct answer is B.** Contour farming involves tilling at right angles to the slope of the land. In this method, small ridges are created that help prevent water from running down the slope and eroding the soil. Choice A is incorrect because it describes strip tillage, which is a method that involves tilling only in the narrow strip that is to receive the seeds. The rest of the soil and any crop residue from the previous year are left undisturbed. Choice C is incorrect because it is describing the method of diversifying cropping systems, which helps supply the soil with a variety of nutrients. Choice D is incorrect because the method of leaving a ridge from the previous year is ridge tillage.

56. **The correct answer is A.** An increase in land developed for agricultural use has caused an increase in soil erosion. Choice B is incorrect because air pollution is not caused by agricultural land use. Choice C is incorrect because agricultural practices helped to increase crop yields. Choice D is incorrect because the Agricultural Revolution didn't cause an increase in pests.

57. **The correct answer is C.** The limiting factor is a condition of an environment that determines the population size of a given organism. Choice A is incorrect because a limiting factor is an environmental influence on the population of an organism, but it doesn't affect fertility rate. Choice B is incorrect because a limiting factor is an extrinsic factor. Choice D is incorrect because the limiting factor is a condition within the environment.

58. **The correct answer is C.** Deforestation worldwide is largely due to the clearing of land for agricultural purposes. Choice A is incorrect because acid rain affects some forests, but most forests are cleared by human activity. Choice B is incorrect because drought is not a usual cause of deforestation. Choice D is incorrect because although forest fires are a cause of deforestation, more forests are cleared for agricultural purposes than affected by forest fires.

59. **The correct answer is C.** In a well-designed sanitary landfill, methane gas is trapped as it is released from the decomposing waste. It can then be used as an energy source. Choice A is incorrect because methane gas, not ethane, is obtained from landfills. Choice B is incorrect because hydrogen is not obtained from a landfill. Choice D is incorrect because steam is obtained from geothermal wells, not landfills.

60. **The correct answer is B.** Desertification occurs most often in regions such as Northern Africa because there is irregular and unpredictable rainfall. Choice A is incorrect because desertification is more prevalent in Northern Africa than the Western United States. Choice C is incorrect because desertification is not a particular problem in Eastern Europe. Choice D is incorrect because Central America receives heavy rainfall.

Printed in the USA
CPSIA information can be obtained
at www.ICGtesting.com
JSHW012043140824
68134JS00033B/3229

9 780768 944440